Edward Berdoe

**Browning's Message to His Time: His Religion, Philosophy, and**

**Science**

Edward Berdoe

**Browning's Message to His Time: His Religion, Philosophy, and Science**

ISBN/EAN: 9783337080914

Printed in Europe, USA, Canada, Australia, Japan

Cover: Foto ©Thomas Meinert / pixelio.de

More available books at **www.hansebooks.com**

# BROWNING'S
# MESSAGE TO HIS TIME:

## *His Religion, Philosophy, and Science.*

BY

## EDWARD BERDOE,

MEMBER OF THE ROYAL COLLEGE OF SURGEONS OF ENGLAND ;
LICENTIATE OF THE ROYAL COLLEGE OF PHYSICIANS (EDINBURGH) ;
MEMBER OF THE BRITISH MEDICAL ASSOCIATION ;
ETC., ETC.

"As the eyes of Lynceus were said to see through the earth, so the poet turns the world to glass, and shows us all things in their right series and procession. For through that better perception, he stands one step nearer to things, and sees the flowing or metamorphosis. . . . The poet alone knows astronomy, chemistry, vegetation, and animation, for he does not stop at these facts, but employs them as signs."—EMERSON ; *The Poet.*

LONDON:

## SWAN SONNENSCHEIN & CO.,
### PATERNOSTER SQUARE.
1890.

# CONTENTS.

# INTRODUCTION.

As I stood by the grave of Mr. Browning in
the Abbey crowded with representative men
and women famous in Art, in Science, and in
Letters, when he was honoured by the nation in
being voted by acclamation a place amongst our
immortals, and welcomed, as it seemed to most
of us, I think, who were present on that grand
and solemn occasion by his peers who seemed
to look down approvingly from their sculptured
tombs, I thought of all the hard things the
thoughtless world had been saying of the great
poet these many years, and how late in coming
were the recognition and honours which cul-
minated in the pomp and dignified ceremony
of that day, and I mused on the lines in his
*Paracelsus*, where the hero says so sadly,—

"'Tis only when they spring to heaven that angels
    Reveal themselves to you ; they sit all day
    Beside you, and lie down at night by you
    Who care not for their presence, muse or sleep,
    And all at once they leave you and you know them !
        We are so fooled, so cheated !"

R. B.                                               B

We have indeed been fooled and cheated out of our rights in Browning's noble verse all these long years. We have permitted wretched scribes, who had no sympathy either with the motive, the method, or the genius of the poet, to tell us,—we were too indolent to see for ourselves,—that this man's work was not poetry at all,—actually took a miserable creature's word, who wrote of *Bells and Pomegranates* the single critical assertion, "rubbish!" and let him write on, nothing heeding, the bravest, most bracing and virile body of literature that has emanated from any English author since Shakespeare. Now we are finding out our mistake, and it is to be feared that our last state will be worse than our first. Browning will become fashionable, everybody will. read him, everybody praise him ; and this will be as uncritical and false as was the previous neglect and contumely.

Several years ago a speaker at one of the meetings of the Browning Society said that "the *students* of Browning would find immediate profit in his works, though those who only read him for amusement would usually be disappointed. He was not anxious to see

Browning 'popular' in the vulgar sense. In the nature of things he never could be popular with the mere reader who does not care to exercise his brains. But if a student would invest thought in his work, he would be a thousand-fold repaid for his venture. What he dreaded was an affectation of admiring Browning without an effort to understand him." The affectation will come soon. It will be idle to maintain that Browning presents no difficulties to his readers; it is, however, still more idle to affirm, as some do, that he is purposely obscure. He does require study, but he will repay it abundantly, which is a great deal more than can be said of many things which occupy intelligent minds. "Lofty mountains," as has been well said, "enshroud their heads with clouds"; and if Browning is often obscure, it must be conceded that his subjects are usually concerned with the deepest problems which agitate the human mind. It is not possible to follow the intricate windings of the human heart in the phraseology and methods which suffice for the ballad, the epic, or the drama of mere action. Browning is always subjective, and probably will never appeal to any great extent except to the class of mind which delights in the analysis of our motives.

Of course this class will gradually widen, for the analysis of human nature and the search after the hidden springs of conduct will grow with the improvement in our methods of education. The fact is, Browning is in advance of his age ; but there are some to whom this will be no objection. He will prove most useful to the large class of thinkers who have broken away from dogmatic Christianity on account of supposed scientific difficulties which stand in the way of their unqualified acceptance. Browning is not only a Theistic poet, but he is a Christian. No Church can label him and pack him away in its cabinet ; but for all that his works bear abundant testimony that the great doctrines of the Christian faith were heartily accepted by him, and accepted upon grounds which seem to many to be more satisfactory than those on which they are generally presented by theologians. He never asks his readers to shut their eyes and open their mouths ; he always says, "Open your eyes, look, see why this is. How good it is that it should be just this way !" " A scientific faith," of course, as he says, "is absurd"; but he gives us so much reasonableness for our belief, that it is in some cases stronger than would be mere cold mathematical proofs, *if* it were possible to obtain such. So catholic were the great poet's sympathies, so all embracing his love for every earnest endeavour after truth and righteousness, that some narrow-minded Christians, as they could not encircle him within their contracted boundaries, have not scrupled to doubt his Christianity. On the other hand, many non-theists profess to find evidence in some passages of his works that the real Browning was not a believer himself, but only spoke dramatically when uttering Christian arguments. Candidly, I must say that I do not believe Browning was enough of a dramatist to escape from himself in any of his poems; and as every one of his characters talks Browning, it follows that a good many Browning thoughts find expression in his works. I have quoted in the following pages passages enough to prove this to all except very hardened theorists. But I have even stronger proof of my contention. Mr. Browning's books had been of such service to my own mind, that I once wrote to acquaint him with the fact, when I received the following letter :—

"19, WARWICK CRESCENT, W.

"*Jan. 12th,* '85.

"DEAR DR. BERDOE,—

"What can I hope to say in return for such sympathy and generous desire to take in the case of my endeavours in poetry—the will for the deed ? I am rewarded over and over again a hundred-fold for whatever pains I have taken by—were it only one—such testimony to their result as goodness like yours chooses to estimate it. All I require acknowledgment for is simply that I have aspired to give effect to my own convictions, and would prefer success in that direction to any other. For your help in this respect, pray believe me,

"Dear Dr. Berdoe,

"Yours gratefully ever,

"ROBERT BROWNING."

If the young men and women of the present day who think that the old religion which nurtured and sustained their parents is no longer adapted to folks who have attended courses of science lectures and taken degrees

Dear Dr Berdoe,

What can I hope to say in return for such sympathy and generous desire to take in the case of my endeavours in poetry - the will for the deed? I am rewarded over and over again a hundred fold for whatever pains I have taken by - were it only one such testimony to their result - as goodness like yours chooses to estimate it. All I require acknowledgement for is simply that I have aspired to give effect to my own convictions and would prefer success in that direction to any other. For your help in this respect, pray believe me, Dear Dr Berdoe,

Yours gratefully ever

Robert Browning

in arts, could be induced to extend their studies so far as to honour our poet, with a few months' attention, I venture to think, they must ultimately at least admit that Christianity has something to say for itself after all, and even that it is not absolutely inconsistent with a science degree to yield obedience to its claims. Our young people, I believe, have given up saying,—

> "Twinkle, twinkle, little star!
> How I wonder what you are!"

Since astronomy and spectroscopic chemistry have become popularized, I am told they say now,—

> "Twinkle, twinkle, little star!
> I don't wonder what you are!
> What you are I know quite well,
> And your component parts can tell!"

These are the sort of persons who would be vastly improved by a course of Browning; and my only feeling of complacency in the advent of the Browning fashion is connected with the conviction that some of these clever young ladies and gentlemen will, before long, have to discover how little they really know after all.

With the exception of one essay in this

volume—that on Rabbi Ben Ezra—the various articles were originally read as papers before the Browning Society, or delivered as lectures to larger audiences. This will account for a phraseology and style which in many places is obviously that of the platform.

I trust I shall not be accused of presumption in offering to a wider public than that for which the following papers were originally intended my thoughts about Mr. Browning's works; but I am impressed with the hope that they may lead some troubled spirits to reconsider their attitude towards the great truths of religion, and to find rest for the weariness of their souls in a return to the faith which is as true and as necessary for the man of science as for the child at its mother's knee.

In several places it will be noticed that there is some slight overlapping in the various papers, and a thought or quotation is now and again repeated. It was not desirable to break the continuity of the thought by excising such passages, especially as they generally present the recurring idea in a slightly different form.

# BROWNING'S MESSAGE TO HIS TIME.

As this nineteenth century draws to its close,
while the struggle between faith and scepticism
has passed into the acute stage ; while our
philosophers and men of science chant peans
over the downfall of creeds and superstitions,
and hail with shouts of joyful anticipation the
coming of the age of science ; while the foundations of orthodoxy are being undermined by
criticism and the study of comparative religions ;
there are not a few anxious souls, who amid all
this destruction are eagerly asking : " What is
to take the place of the banished faith ?   What
are we going to write on the *tabula rasa* the
end of the century will have left us ?   How are
we going to teach our children ?   How rule
the people ?   Is the moral law Divine, and are
its sanctions eternal ? or may we change our
ideas of what is right and wrong, as a railway
company varies its bye-laws ? "

A sad picture has been drawn in a recent
review of a possible " faithless world," with its

"belittling of life," and its gospel of despair.
It has been said the picture is an impossible
one; but those who have studied the question
most deeply seem to think it will sooner or
later be realized in fact.   In the beautiful words
of Matthew Arnold,—

> " The sea of faith
> Was once, too, at the full, and round earth's shore
> Lay like the folds of a bright girdle furled ;
> But now I only hear
> Its melancholy, long, withdrawing roar,
> Retreating, to the breath
> Of the night wind, down the vast edge's drear
> And naked shingles of the world."

"Go into a London club, listen to the talk of
men of the world on moral questions, and see
how little of earnest faith in any moral law is
left among them.   Compare the talk with
what it was twenty-five years ago.   Then it
was an offence to affect doubt of any fundamental principle of orthodoxy.  'To express
unbelief was to invite insult; to assume that
your neighbour could be anything but an orthodox Christian was to affront him.   Now-a-
days even conservative society rather patronizes
religion than believes in it, and a similar scepticism prevails on points of morality.   A man

may to-day affirm that marriage is an ab-
surdity, may challenge the first principles of
social order, might have defended murder till
the assassinations committed by Land Leaguers
and Nihilists frightened society into a passion
on that subject,—may argue against any of the
ten commandments, and will be answered in
almost equal terms."

Such is the indictment against our time
which a recent essayist puts into the mouth
of one of his characters in a controversy on
Negative Science and Natural Ethics (Percy
Greg, *Without God*, p. 169).

A short time since I had a letter from Berlin
about Mr. Browning's new book, *Ferishtah's
Fancies*, from an eminent man of letters, in
which the following passage occurs : "If I am
irresistibly impelled to hate the evil, cruelty,
brutality of the world, what consolation is there
in telling me about its Creator and Perpetuator,
unless it be to make me hate Him ? Browning
needs a limited God for dramatic purposes ; a
God selling Himself to Satan, but an omnipotent God for metaphysical purposes. He cannot have both. For myself, I have, as you
know, been compelled to leave my religion in

the only certainty that is left me—the certainty
that justice, kindness, love, are good, and the
only evidences of good in the universe. But
as they are not so strong in the earth as in-
justice and inhumanity, how can I say they are
omnipotent in the universe? 'They may be,'
but how can I build on a 'perhaps' I have not
been able to find? (As if all our life we were
not just doing that!) When I can find a man
or woman who can show me a higher type of
God than some crucified or mendicant lover of
men, I shall believe in Omnipotence."

To talk like this has become the fashion of
the day, not only with our writers in magazines
and reviews, but with the students of our
colleges and the half-educated youth of both
sexes. Canon Liddon, in a sermon at St.
Paul's, said lately :—

"An acknowledgment of Christ too often
was met with a delicate curl of the lip, a gentle
shrug of the shoulder, a scarcely perceptible
raising of the eyebrows, which were more
terrible to some young men than to have to
lead their regiment across a plain swept by
the enemy's cannon. These expressive atti-
tudes were meant to say, 'You do not mean

to tell me that at this time of day you believe these old fables?' These sneers," Canon Liddon continued, " which did their work with such fatal effect, represented not superior knowledge, not high moral principle, not complex superiority, but were the extract or essence of a certain form of class opinion, or rather section or subsection of opinion, the holders of which wish to establish without argument the idea that Christ had had His day."

The Canon then gave an account of a dinner party at the West End fifty years' ago, where, when the ladies had retired, the conversation, under the direction of one of the gentlemen, took a turn utterly derogatory to Jesus Christ. A guest asked his host's permission to ring the bell, and when the servant came ordered his carriage, saying with the courtesy of perfect self-command that he was sorry that he was obliged to retire, but that he was still a Christian. This act of simple courage was that, not of a bishop or clergyman, but of the great Minister of the early part of Queen Victoria's reign—Sir Robert Peel. The preacher pointed out that while Christians were

less and less courageous, more and more fasti-
dious, so afraid of being too enthusiastic, and
so engaged in weighing or mincing their words,
every conceivable blasphemy, folly, and nega-
tion of the truth appeared in the press, and was
discussed in society, while error, moral and
intellectual, stalked everywhere, now loudly
advertising, now gently insinuating itself.

That some half-a-dozen eminent English
men of science have cast off what they are
pleased to term the trammels of superstition,
and at the same time live pure and noble lives,
does not for a moment prove that the great
mass of ignorant mankind can be decent members of society, good fathers and mothers,
and worthy citizens, without faith in God, the
existence of the soul and the conscience. A few
philosophers may succeed in doing this, though
neither Voltaire nor Rousseau nor, indeed, any
others of whom we have complete information,
as far as I can gather, led lives that would for
a moment compare with the purity, gentleness,
modesty, and beauty of those led under the
eyes of us all by simple folk nurtured in the
faith we talk so lightly about parting with for
ever. Many prophets have come amongst us

and spoken great truths to us. The voice of
Carlyle has only just ceased, with that of
Emerson, to rebuke our shams and our low-
mindedness ; while that of Ruskin still cries
aloud for truth and reality and earnest, honest
heart in work and word.

But there is one prophet who has none of
Carlyle's bitterness and distempered views of
life, none of Ruskin's far-fetched theories and
impracticable mediævalism, none of Emerson's
vapoury transcendentalism, so beautiful to contemplate, so hard to condense into anything
usable—Robert Browning, well described by the
founder of the Browning Society as " the manliest, the strongest, the life-fullest, the deepest
and thoughtfullest living poet, the one poet
needing earnest study, and the one most worthy
of it." *

I once heard Mr. Russell Lowell say,
' Browning is the poet who stays by one
longest." From the comparatively few persons
who are lovers or admirers of Browning, though
the circle is a daily widening one, it may per-

---

* Dr. Furnivall, in the inaugural address to the Browning
Society.

haps be surmised by the inconsiderate, that
either he is not understandable or not worth the
trouble of understanding. Doubtless, every one
has met advocates of both of these theories.
It is getting a little too late in the day, however, to be able to take refuge in the latter
suggestion, which even the *Saturday Review*
has had to abandon ; and the only excuse one
hears much of now from those who are not
Browning's admirers is the former, that he is
too obscure, too involved, too rugged, to make
anything of. One of our most eminent living
women of letters, whom I asked to write a
paper for the Browning Society, recently declared to me she had tried to understand our
poet, but could make nothing of him, and
added : "When I am tired and want my mind
refreshing, I like to put my head down into a
great big cabbage-rose like Tom Moore ; and
you urge me to bury my nose in a bunch of
thistles like Browning." Now, I have come to
the conclusion, that much of this talk of the obscurity of Browning is affectation, simply a form
of cant. I do not use the term offensively, but
in the sense Webster gives : " The phraseology
of a sect used without sincerity." People who

declare that *In Memoriam* presents no difficulty to them at all, make wry faces at *Paracelsus, La Saisiaz*, or *Fifine*, and say it is no
use trying, it is all beyond them, and worse
than the higher mathematics. Browning has a
sorrowful line which we should blush to read.

> " Ye British public who like me not,
> God love you, whom I yet have laboured for."

And in one of his poems he very caustic-
ally compares the great poets of England,—
Shakespeare, Milton, Spenser,—to butts of
precious wine, that stand in our cellars but are
rarely tasted. We swear by them, he says, but
how much have we had out of the casks ?
You know this is not a very honest age, it
would hardly do to speak ill of Shakespeare
and Milton and Spenser ; but, after all, how
many glasses have we had out of these butts ?

I have met many who have read Browning
once, and did not like him. I have met some
who have read him twice, and said the same ;
while those who took the trouble to read him
over and over again, found their profit in the
labour.

Precious stones do sometimes want digging

R. B.                                        C

for.   Diamonds and nuggets are not always to
be stumbled across on the footpath.   Pickaxes
and crushing mills are not unknown in mining
operations ; and the treasures of kings are kept
in strong boxes.   The bee cannot gather his
honey from the simplest flower without con-
tributing his quota to the processes of fertilization ; and the stimulation of our thinking faculties is no small part of the good which great
teachers have to do for us.   The quartz will
pay for crushing, the diamond for digging.   By
the nature of the treasure we expect a certain
trouble in getting it.   Some one cleverly said,
" Browning treats obscure subjects deeply, not
deep subjects obscurely."   When we remember
that he discourses on the great problems of life
and mind, that his songs are of soul struggles
and the birth-throes of great thoughts, we shall
not expect them to be clothed in language of a
love song, or the words that befit a hymn to
a daisy.

Carlyle somewhere complains, " How loth we
are to read great works !   How much more
willingly we cross our legs, back to candle,
feet to fire, with some *Pickwick* or lowest
trash of that nature !   The reason is, we are

very indolent, very wearied and forlorn, and read oftenest chiefly that we may forget ourselves."

One difficulty about Browning, I may mention in passing, is the intensely concentrated form in which all his great thoughts are cast. This, it has been remarked, is the tendency of all the greatest writers of the age ; they suggest rather than vapour, they compress instead of being diffuse, and take for granted that we can do without platitude, often giving their readers credit for more knowledge than they possess. This latter charge, I admit, *can* often be fairly brought against Browning. If you were familiar with the Encyclopædia as with a horn-book, you would have all your work cut out to keep up with him; and he seems to expect this of us rather too rashly. You can't read him for mere after-dinner amusement, as you take up Thomson's *Seasons* or Cowper's *Task ;* but if you take his *Paracelsus*, the *Inn Album*, or indeed any of the earlier poems except *Sordello*, with the attention you would expect to give to an article in the *Quarterly*, you shall rise from the study a manlier man, a stronger and more earnest seeker after the true, the noble, and the good, than when you first opened the page. You will be braced as the traveller who leaves the hot, dry plains for the mountain heights.

But we do not invite you only to snow-clad altitudes, we do not want to bury you on Alpine heights.

Every line of Browning is stamped with his strong personality. He is nothing if not virile, as becomes a man with a message for a limp and gelatinous age. He is analytical and subjective in a most marked degree, as becomes a teacher of an age of science.

All his students say, " How strong he is!" One feels he is safe to trust—a Mr. Greatheart in a world whose leaders seem weak-kneed beside him. While the religious teachers of the day are lamenting the decay of faith in the first principles of religion, and the very idea of a divine revelation has become repugnant to so many, Browning, holding no brief from any of the Churches, comes forward to boldly call the science and philosophy of the day back to religion, declaring that Love,—God's love,—is the only thing that can keep the intellect of man from madness, as the brain must cease to perform its work efficiently when the heart's work is imperfectly done. He re-states Christianity on its earliest, simplest, and too forgotten lines, contests the ground for an exalted Theism of the noblest kind, and proclaims that the great truths of Christianity rest upon philosophical and scientific foundations, that though the superstructures built on them by some Churches and some theologians are too often weak and rotten, the great truths of God, the soul, and the future life remain amid all the storm of adverse criticism unharmed by a single wave that has beaten upon them.

With the truest sympathy with all the doubts and difficulties of belief, he invites us to follow him on a path with whose every turn he is familiar.

> "Rather I prize the doubt low kinds exist without,
> Finished and finite clods untroubled by a spark."

I know no thinker on religious subjects so worthy of confidence as he, because he is well abreast of all the scientific thought of the age. Few even of Browning's closest students are aware how thoroughly imbued with science he is ; and though I believe that the poet is the natural king of men,—

"A poet must be earth's essential king,"

as he says himself,—he is so much the more
a king when he is master of all his subjects'
needs.

He feels quite sure that, although our processes of thought are perhaps due to certain
definite molecular changes in the grey matter
of our brain, which abstract so much of the
sulphates and phosphates from its blood supply,
these changes are not the thought itself, as
the Materialist claims.

You will not easily | blind Robert Browning
with a handful of physiological dust, nor daze
him with a show of chemical formulæ. He
knows just as much about physiology and
natural science in general as the Materialist and
Agnostic; and he tells you that neither their
scalpel, their crucible, nor their microscope
have brought us the least step nearer to finding
out the mystery of being—

"To know of, think about—
Is all man's sum of faculty effects
When exercised on earth's least atom, Son !
What was, what is, what may such atom be ?
No answer !  Still, what seems it to man's sense ?
An atom with some certain properties
Known about, thought of as occasion needs,

—Man's—but occasions of the universe?
Unthinkable, unknowable to man."
*Ferishtah's Fancies*, p. 131.

One of the chief characteristics of a great
poet, is a very high development of the faculty
of observation. To bring that faculty to perfection, there must be added an acquaintance with
almost the whole sum of human knowledge.
In writing a paper on Browning as a scientific
poet, I have been amazed at the vastness of
the field of human knowledge explored by our
great poet. Be sure, therefore, that if he is a
Christian poet, as he certainly is, he can give
the world very cogent reasons for the faith
that is in him. Such a teacher at such an
epoch has a message for his time of peculiar
force and significance. If the world, turning its
back on the altar and the pulpit, has steadfastly
faced anything now-a-days, it is the Professor's
Desk, of which it asks, " Who will show us any
good ? " I think the voice from that chair of
science will more and more clearly pronounce
in favour of Christianity. It has already done so
in Germany, where the highest thought is no
longer agnostic or sceptical ; and I see in the
whole scientific thought of Browning, and the

way in which he is influencing the highest
intellect of our country, marked evidence that
"the watery swell of rationalism is going
down" here also. Did I startle you when I
read that terrible indictment of my atheistic
correspondent from Berlin, who, because he sees
a very imperfect world, denies the existence of
a perfect Creator and Perpetuator? I could
reassure you out of Browning, who in a
hundred noble passages tells us that the evil,
and cruelty, and hate, and vice, and pain in the
world are not purposeless, as they perhaps seem
to our limited knowledge.

All this dread machinery of pain and sorrow,
he believes,—or he would otherwise be confounded by it,—was devised to evolve the moral
qualities of man, and "wring from out all pain
all pleasure for a common heritage." As the
crystals branch where the salt marshes stagnate,
as blood dries to crimson, so in every shape is
evil beautified—after all, evil is a result not less
natural than good, it must therefore have a
purpose. This is a low reason, perhaps; he
gives us a higher one—evil must stay for men's
own account,—

"For mankind springs

> Salvation by each hindrance interposed,
> They climb."

Living itself, properly understood, is made up of good and evil. Failure may be, after all, only apparent. His optimism is so far-reaching that, contemplating the corpses in the Morgue, he can say that he hopes—

> " That what began best, can't end worst,
> Nor what God blest once, prove accurst."

We can only see the goodness of God by means of evil, only appreciate the serenity of heaven through the noises of earth, only win our souls by fighting the wrongs and pains of life. God's love is at issue still with sin visibly when any wrong is done on earth. There is a need for sin and death,—happily only a transient one,— there is Power sufficient for righting all the wrongs of life, and through Love the power will be resumed.

Amelioration is the dominant note of Nature, the lily is the evolution of a grass; the monstrous and terrible forms of giant strength that wandered through the mists of the half-cooled earth, ages before the advent of man,—

> " When dragons in their prime
> Tare each other in their slime,"—

have long since given place to gentler forms,
and the earth is no longer held in subjection by
the muscle and giant bone of the megatherium,
but by the convolutions of the human brain.
What this world may yet become, may be in
some slight degree imagined if we in fancy
transport ourselves to those distant ages of the
past before the advent of man, and compare its
condition when hideous monsters roamed its
tangled forests with the present age of civiliza-
tion. May we not hope that the hateful forms
of vice, cruelty, disease, and sin, may, like the
extinct monsters of past geological periods,
disappear before the softening influence of
virtue, knowledge, and love ? Browning finds
reason for such a hope in a similar reflection.

> " Dragons were and serpents are,
> And blindworms will be ; ne'er emerged
> Any new-created Python for man's
> Plague since earth was purged."
>
> *La Saisiaz*, p. 57.

We must never forget in this relation, that a
very large proportion of the evil in the world
arises from violation of the moral law, written
plainly in the conscience of man. Browning
says, If you break the law of gravity, you must

not complain that the air does not hold you up
when you step over a precipice. Just so with
moral evil. If you will be lazy and vicious, you
mustn't grumble at being poor and ill. It is
simply a question of cause and effect.

We have liberty of doing evil, that our doing
good may have a grace. Nature's law is very
simple : such effects succeed such causes.
Heaven and hell depend upon man's deed on
earth just as certainly as you make point meet
point or miss it by the straightness or crooked-
ness of the line you draw between them. If
you want to live on earth, draw your breath ; if
you want to have eternal life, be just! Death
in either case results from breach of law.

Browning's conception of God is a very
noble one. He *sees* God in the immensities, he
*feels* His love in his heart. God stands away
a hairbreadth off—

" To give room for the newly made to live."

Man is able to grieve, but able also to glorify
God, as no mere machine could do—

"Made perfect as a thing of course."

With him evil is always the accident.

" This is the note of evil, for good lasts."

In the darkest life he sees reason for hope. In the most criminal soul he detects the potentialities for good.

> "Progress is man's distinctive mark alone,
>   Not God's, and not the beast's : God is, they are,
>   Man partly is, and wholly hopes to be."
>                       *A Death in the Desert.*

Is the whole world groaning under its load of pain ? He says,—

> "Put pain from out the world, what room were left
> . For thanks to God, for love to Man ?   Why thanks,—
>   Except for some escape, whate'er the style,
>   From pain that might be, name it as thou mayst?"

Browning's idea of God, as might be expected from so subjective a poet, is largely abstract. Not that he opposes the concrete conception of the Divine Personality as revealed in the Bible, but because, valuable as the anthropomorphic Hebrew idea of God was, the larger and wider our thought of the Supreme Being becomes, the healthier and more ennobling it will be for mankind. For a world emerging from fetish worship and Polytheism it was a vast stride to arrive at, that one anthropomorphic God; and, notwithstanding all the scoffing of anti-theistic or a-theistic opponents,

that Hebrew Javeh was a most elevated conception, the highest the mind of the time was
able to bear. Is the world ready, even yet, for
a perfectly pure faith?

In the character of Pompilia, in *The Ring
and the Book*, he has portrayed how the soul of
his heroine was made perfect through suffering,
and shows how a mere child, ignorant of the
world and all its ways, with neither advantages
of home, education, or any congenial surroundings, through suffering, and suffering only,
leaped all at once from the mere animal existence to all the grace, the dignity, and beauty
of the highest type of womanhood, as the
chrysalis, in one bright hour, from the dull earth
below, bursts into the summer air with gold
and glory on its wings. The poor murdered
creature sees how suffering has raised her—

> "One cannot both have and not have, you know,—
> Being right now, I am happy, and colour things."

sees the good of suffering when she hears God
say—

> "Bear! not stand by, bear to see My angels bear";

and owns that though—

> "In His face is light,
> But in His shadow healing too,"

she does not think less of God for being crucified or mendicant, but says :—

"I never realized God's birth before—
How He grew likest God in being born."

Dr. Furnivall has well described our poet as
the "healthfullest" of the day.  It is very true ;
and the man or woman who aspires to teach
anything to this century must first of all be
*healthful.*

I think the day has gone by when poets of
unsound mind have much in them to bless the
world with.  This man has a sound mind in a
sound body.  Hear him.  Of course, being a
scientific poet, he is an Optimist.  The Evolutionist shows us how animal and vegetable
life tend to higher and more beautiful forms,
especially under cultivation.  He is compelled,
to a large extent, to be optimistic.

Schopenhauer declared life to be utterly un-
desirable, and painted all the operations of
Nature in the darkest colours of his gloomy
palette, yet one who records a visit to him at
home says he did not find the great Pessimist
sitting in sackcloth and ashes, contemplating
how best to terminate the miseries of his existence, but enjoying life and all its good things

in a beautiful home with artistic surroundings, and under conditions generally calculated to make it an enviable one. Browning lives as he teaches. He is not touched with the faintest trace of unhealthy pessimism.

Second to no student of Tennyson in my admiration for his *magnum opus*, the *In Memoriam*, and alive as I am to the un-wisdom of making invidious comparisons between two such master-minds, I cannot forbear in illustration of my subject, contrasting the *In Memoriam* of Tennyson for his friend Hallam, with the poem on very similar lines, *La Saisiaz*, of Browning in memory of a lady friend who died in Brittany : the former a threnody, almost a woman's wail over her own heart sorely lacerated by death's severance ; the latter a noble psalm of victory of soul over matter and of hope beyond the grave.

If any one doubts Dr. Furnivall's claim, that " Browning is the manliest, strongest, life-fullest, deepest, thoughtfullest of our living writers," let him contrast these two In Memoriams.

To thine own self be true ; he is never tired of emphasizing this !

"Weakness never needs be falseness : truth is truth in each
    degree
Thunder-pealed by God to Nature, whispered by my soul
    to me."

*La Saisiaz*, p. 24.

I have in this lecture endeavoured to indicate some of the salient points of Browning's
message.   I think I have shown that his great
thoughts shine over the troubled seas of speculative thought as a Pharos, whose light is strong
and clear enough for our greatest needs.   In
the many extracts I have read, you will not
have failed to notice abundant evidence of his
manly, strong, life-full, thoughtful, deep personality.   If I have adduced any reasons to
lead to a closer, more earnest acquaintance with
him on the part of any here present, I hope
they will not be deterred by the prevalent idea
of his obscurity, but go boldly to work and
fetch out the precious treasures for themselves—
they do not lie so very far below the surface—
I think he answers some of the deep question-
ings of the soul.   It is hard to have to traverse
the dark ways of life with no other light than
the ignis fatuus of our own reason.   When the
end comes, may we all say with his Paracelsus :

" If I stoop into a dark tremendous sea of cloud,
  It is but for a time; I press God's lamp
  Close to my breast; its splendour, soon or late,
  Will pierce the gloom : I shall emerge one day ! "

## APPENDIX.

THE following observations, taken from the transactions of the Browning Society, on the relation of
Browning to the nineteenth century, were made from
the chair at the meeting of the Society on Friday,
April 27th, 1888, when—

MISS WHITEHEAD read a paper on Robert Browning as a poet of the nineteenth century, its interests
and influences, practical and metaphysical.

DR. BERDOE said that he was sure he expressed
the feeling of the meeting in very heartily thanking
Miss Whitehead for her valuable paper. He had
listened to it with great satisfaction, partly for its
own inherent merits, and partly because Miss Whitehead had shown how thoroughly she had studied
Browning, and had given so much of his best thought
in his own words. A very difficult question had been
dealt with, " The Relation of Browning to the Nineteenth Century." He took it that it was necessary for
a poet of this age to be in sympathy with its aspirations, its work, and its need. How far Mr. Browning
had met these requirements had often been discussed
by that Society; and he hoped Miss Whitehead's
paper would enable them to discuss it profitably on

R. B.                                                    D

this occasion. The principal aspiration of the age was a passionate longing for truth, combined with a purity of intention and a reverence of method in truth-seeking, such as, he ventured to say, had never been equalled in any age. It was an age of science, but an age of faith in its sublimest and noblest aspect, an age of destruction if they would; but amidst the ruins of the temples of the past he thought they saw already laid the foundations of the great Religion of Humanity. Then the work of the age was to love. the weak, to counteract the ,cruel law of Nature, that only the strongest shall survive—not always, of course, the strongest in muscle and bone—the strongest in brain. An age of humanism, an age which had literally taken some of the sting from death, and some of the terrors from the grave. Let them think for a moment how great were the needs of this age, what an uprising of millions asking for mental food! The liberated slaves of feudal ages, now happily passing away. What a field for scattering great thoughts! What did we specially want in this age, this age of rush, and turmoil, and bustle? We wanted a purer faith, a worthier philosophy, a higher standard of rectitude, deeper springs of conduct, more reality, less sham. Browning helped us in these aims. Look at the works from which quotations had been given —*Christmas Eve, Ferishtah's Fancies, Paracelsus,* and *Parleyings.* There never was so much desire to benefit our fellow-men as at present, a feeling, it must be admitted, not largely the outcome of the Christian Church, but of those who had separated themselves

from her. Not that this was the fault of the Church,
but the fault of those who misinterpreted and misunderstood its mission. Some of the noblest minds
worked for humanity outside the Church; but that
was not the fault of the Gospel. Was there any
poetry to be got out of a consideration of the aspirations and work of the present age? Walt Whitman
said there was; and whatever they thought of Walt
Whitman as a poet—and as Browningites they must
not be too hard on him—he was certainly a great
thinker. Ruskin said we were crushing all the poetry
out of the earth, but he (Dr. Berdoe) did not think
so. With all the rush and whirl he thought there
was plenty of poetry; there was poetry in the Chan-
nel tunnel and the St. Gothard railway. He thought
sometimes, when he read *Christmas Eve*, that that
mantle of Christ meant the means of locomotion at
the present day. As we saw more of the world, and
mixed with our fellow-men, we got some of our pre-
judices rubbed down, and our angles taken off. Mr.
Browning's teaching was, that we should get a little
more humility, and a trifle less conceit with our science.
The great objection to the science of the age was its
want of reverence and love. The great teaching of
Paracelsus was, that neither love without knowledge,
nor knowledge without love will do; and the message
for the age was, that with all the knowledge we had,
we wanted more love to everything that breathes,
that lives and suffers. Perhaps some there would
laugh at Mr. Browning's views on vivisection; he
did not at all think a scientific audience would accept

Browning's teaching on that point, but let them remember that if they called him and those who held
with Mr. Browning foolish and ignorant, that Balaam's
ass saw what the prophet riding upon it could not
see, and they might be right after all.    Religion with
Mr. Browning was put upon a basis that the intelligent thinking people of the age could accept.    Mr.
Fotheringham said, that religion is a part of the vital
study of man.    This paper had opened up a good
many questions for discussion.    He called upon Dr.
Furnivall to continue the discussion.

# THE RELIGION OF ROBERT BROWNING.

THERE is a beautiful dream-story in one of Jean Paul Richter's *Flower, Fruit, and Thorn Pieces*. A philosopher has been discussing the existence of God, and that "with as little feeling as most of us grant it." Musing on the pros and cons of the question, he falls asleep, and dreams that he awakes in a churchyard, the graves are unclosed, and shadows stalk erect in the gloom. Avalanches fall and earthquakes rend the rocks.

The great church is overthrown, and round its ruined altar the ghosts of the departed congregate in silence and awe. A lofty, sable form, having the expression of a never-ending sorrow, sinks from above upon the altar, and all the dead exclaim, "Christ! is there no God?" And he answered, "There is none!" He tells how he traversed the worlds, ascended into the suns, and flew with the milky way through the wilderness of the heavens, he gazed into the immeasurable depths of the abyss and cried,

"Father, where art Thou?" and no answer
came but from the eternal storm which no one
rules. He looked above for the Divine Eye,
and saw but an empty, bottomless socket,
Eternity lay brooding upon Chaos! The pale
shadows cast themselves before the Christ; they
cry in their unutterable despair, "Jesus! have
we no Father?" and with streaming eyes he
answers, "We are all orphans, I and you; we
are without a Father." Are we really all
orphans? Are we in very truth without the
All-Father? Scientific men say we are, and
they ought to know. They have great telescopes
and they look into the heavens; and they have
powerful microscopes, and they look into the
dust; and they say He is not there. And they
are analysts, and chemists, and physiologists,
and they say there is no room for God at all,
and they can explain everything without Him.
We go to the top of Mount Sinai, and find it
is a howling waste; and out into the lonely
deserts, and we cry aloud, and the eternal
silences are unbroken save by the voice of the
thunder, and we know all about thunder now,
and no God answers us. God is not hidden in
the eternal snows nor in the clouds. The pro-

cesses of life and the worlds of being are daily becoming easier to understand, and the verdict of science is—We are all orphans! So, as there is no God, there can be no religion to bind us to Him, and consequently every man is a law unto himself, and is only answerable to society, which restrains him from doing that which is inconvenient to his fellow-men ; for the rest— eat, drink, and be merry, for to-morrow we die! and we perish as the beasts. This is what nineteenth-century thought proposes to put in place of the Churches, when they are explained out of existence, and for the old faiths when folks have cast them off with other old-world superstitions. But let us see if the case is really as bad as it appears upon the surface. Is everything gone because the first chapter of Genesis is proved to be merely an allegorical poem, because the Bible after all turns out to be but a collection of sacred books like any other row of ancient classics on a student's shelf? Some historical, some poetical, some ethical, considerably inferior to Homer, Shake-speare, and the Bhagavad-gita for practical purposes, as they tell us. Are we then to have no religion, nothing to .bind us to anything higher than self, and nothing to teach our children when they ask us those awkward questions they are so apt to put? " Yes," I hear some of you say. We can make a sacred anthology from the philosophy, the teaching of the sages, and the maxims of the wise men of all ages ; these will help us to live righteously and soberly. And go back to Paganism? which some men say was, at least in Greece, brighter and more beautiful than Christianity ; but which, divested of fine phrases and imported sentiments, we know very well, was simply the worship of very coarse and very sensual and degrading ideas. No ; it is not so bad as that. If we fail to find God in the mountain defiles, or to hear Him in the voices of the thunder ; if we cannot search Him out with our telescopes or see Him in the atoms, there is one place where He will always be found, where He, whatever He be, for none can name Him, dwells eternally—in the heart of man. Oh, students of religion, faithful seekers after truth, ponder this when tempted to discard the Christian conception of God. " The progress of reason was fatal only to the false gods. The true God of the universe, the one God, whom men adore

when they do a good deed, or when they seek
the truth, or when they advise their fellow-men
aright," says Renan, "is established for all
eternity."

I commend to such truth-seekers the religion of Robert Browning, because I think
it is peculiarly helpful to souls in our time.
You know the old philosophers said, the bane
and the antidote grow side by side. You
get fever in the tropical forests of Peru ; but
the bark which cures it is found hard by the
fever spots. Now, it is always thus with speculations and destructive criticisms in all great
crises of thought. It can only be the false
which perishes ; the good must be eternal. It
is good that we have lost so much of the vin-
dictive theology of the past. It is good that
the fogs are dispelled which hid so long from us
our Father's face ; good that we are beginning
to see that Brummagem theologians have only
lost the gods which they made in their own
workshops, and that the God of nature, the
God which dwells in the human heart, the
Spirit of God, the Soul of the world, is reigning
and ruling and loving still. In Robert Browning we are introduced to a religion which is not

a sectarian religion, is not a professional formula, but is just the reasonable belief of a great
English nineteenth-century thinker, who is in
sympathy with all the science and progress and
mental activity and inquiry of our day. We
have outgrown some of our false conceptions
about God, you know; the crude notions about
the Deity formed when man first emerged from
a state of savagery will not do for the men of
to-day. Not that God alters, but our conceptions of Him must grow with the expansion
of our own minds. Robert Browning is an
aged man, but still full of life and vigour, and
I venture to say the greatest philosophical
thinker living. He has been writing poems for
over fifty years, and men are just beginning to
read and value them. It is the stupid fashion
to pretend that he is difficult to understand.
Well, perhaps if we only bring to the task the
amount of brain necessary to enjoy an ordinary
novel with, he may be unintelligible; but as he
deals with deep subjects he demands true study.
Now he has formed certain definite convictions
about God, the soul, and the future state which
he holds very firmly, and which are good for us
to weigh well, because they come from a thinker,

an explorer into the dark recesses of the human
soul, and who is entitled to speak to us in the
name of the science of our day, for he is fully
conversant with it. What does he say about
God, a supreme Being who is over Nature and
pervading her throughout? Well, for one thing,
he thinks that—

> "God dwells in all,
> From life's minute beginnings up at last
> To man."

All nature to Browning is viewed. as a thought
of God. " God is the perfect Poet," he says,
" who in His Person acts His own creations."
So the whole universe is a crystallized thought
of God to him. Within the· past few years
philosophers have told us a great deal more
about the atoms and molecules than we ever
knew before ; and the infinitely little has now
become to its students the awful and incomprehensible. These atoms are " the foundation
stones of the material universe, which, amid
the wreck of composite matter, remain unbroken
and unworn." Of the atoms, Professor Tyndall,
who knows more about them than perhaps any-
body else, says, " they are so small, and, when
grouped to molecules, are so tightly clasped to-

gether, that they are capable of tremors equal in rapidity to those of light and radiant heat " ; " They can vibrate to and fro millions of millions of times in a second." Knowing all this, what does Browning say ? He says,—

> " The small becomes the dreadful and immense."

> " We find great things are made of little things ;
> And little things go lessening, till at last
> Comes God behind them."

Talk about understanding nature, common-sense science, and all the rest of it ! Professor Tyndall, whom men call an atheist, says on this, " I should be inclined to ascribe the creation of the world of molecules to inspiration, rather than to what is known as common sense."

When you want to reach the limits of the understanding, do not take a telescope, and try to penetrate the infinite distances of the stars. Think of the eternal dance of the atoms that never grow old, and which never tire. Think how they may " despise " us, as the poet says.

" I am a materialist," said one to me the other day."

" Oh ! are you ? " I said. " Then tell me all about the atoms."

" The name," says Browning,

> " comes close
> Behind a stomach-cyst, the smallest
> Of creations,"

alluding to the fact that, with all our physiology and our chemistry, we have not, in the
very least, bridged the infinite gulf which
separates living from not-living matter. We
are as far off as ever from understanding how
the lowest form of organic life is generated
from inorganic matter.

" The undevout astronomer is mad." What
do you say to the scoffer and the flippant in the
presence of the atoms ? When Mr. Browning
thinks of the human heart with all its noble and
generous impulses, of the mother's love, and
the martyr's heroism, he does not think of the
vibrations and thrills of so much matter. To
him, as Carlyle said of Frederick the Great,
" it was flatly inconceivable that intellect and
moral emotion could have been put into him
by an entity that had none of its own."

No! He says,—

> " Have I knowledge ? Confounded, it shrivels at wisdom
> laid bare.
> Have I forethought ? How purblind, how blank to the
> infinite care ! "

> "God is seen God
> In the star, in the stone, in the flesh, in the soul, and the
>     clod.
> And then looking within and around me, I ever renew,
> (With that stoop of the soul which, in bending, upraises
>     it too),
> The submission of man's nothing-perfect to God's all-
>     complete,
> As by each new obeisance in spirit, I climb to His feet."

Now, as we can question about all this, and
get our answer, Mr. Browning says,—

> " Question, answer, presuppose
> Two points :. that the thing itself which questions, answers—
>     *is*, it knows,
> As it also knows the thing perceived outside itself—a force,
> Actual ere its own beginning, operative through its course,
> Unaffected by its end—that this thing likewise needs must
>     be.
> Call this—God, then, call that—soul, and both—the only
>     facts for me.
> Prove them facts ?  That they o'erpass my power of prov-
>     ing, proves them such."

So we see that Mr. Browning may be well
described in two of his own lines,—

> "Crowned by prose and verse, and wielding with Wit's
>     bauble, Learning's rod,
> He at least believes in soul, and is very sure of God ! "

Oh! but, you say, what sort of a God ?  Dr.
Martineau has beautifully spoken of the God in

whom he believes as "the Mind that meditates
in beauty and speaks in law." Do not you think
it eminently reasonable that the universe should
have a mind ? Its order is so perfect, that if
there be no God, no central, guiding Spirit, we
are confronted by a vastly greater difficulty
than that presented by the orthodox conception of the order of the universe. But you say,
" When I look around me, and see all the evil,
cruelty, and brutality in the world, what consolation is there in telling me about its Creator,
unless it be to make me hate Him ? " Because,
if God is omnipotent, He could stop all this
evil at a word. I shall let Mr. Browning
answer you. Our poet is, I think, extremely
helpful with his problem of evil in the world.
He is evidently of that school of philosophy
known as the Mystics ; and it is pretty certain
that much of the mysticism pervading European
religious thought had its origin in Buddhism.
If we take the Bhagavad-gita, that beautiful old
Indian book of philosophy, and compare it with
Thomas à Kempis's *Imitation of Christ*, we
cannot fail to be struck by their similarity. To
what extent we owe some of our best religious
thought to Buddhism will never be known, but

it is certain that Mr. Browning has absorbed some of its teaching. Take his view of the evil in the world. He says, in that wonderful poem of his which I commend heartily to every lover of music, the poem called *Abt Vogler*—

"There shall never be one lost good ! What was, shall live
  as before ;
The evil is null, is nought, is silence implying sound ;
What was good, shall be good, with, for evil, so much good
  more ;
On the earth the broken arcs ; in the heaven, a perfect
  round."

The Buddhist, the Mystic, and the Christian philosophers alike agree in denying the reality of evil, and affirming the reality and permanence of good. The direct tendency of all evil is to perish, of all good to become permanent. Walt Whitman beautifully expresses this. He says : " Roaming in thought over the universe, I saw the little that is Good steadily hastening towards immortality, and the vast all that is called Evil I saw hastening to merge itself and become lost and dead."

Mr. Browning goes much further than this, however, and declares :

"In this first
Life, I see the good of evil, why our world began at worst :

Since time means amelioration, tardily enough displayed,
Yet a mainly onward moving, never wholly retrograde.
We know more though we know little, we grow stronger
  though still weak,
Partly see though all too purblind, stammer though we
  cannot speak."

The troubles and pains of life are held by our poet to be necessary for the evolution and development of our highest nature. Says Dr. Martineau : " A world without a contingency or an agony could have had no hero and no saint." Let me tell you an instance of this heroism.

I was called the other day to see a man suffering for the fifth or sixth time from the disease known as lead poisoning, consequent upon working in a lead factory. As I approached his bed, on which he was lying in great agony, I gently reproached him for having returned to such dangerous work after the previous illnesses of the same kind for which I had treated him.

"You will certainly kill yourself," I said.

He replied, looking round on his wife and four little children, " I know that, sir ! Better to risk *that* than that these should starve ! "

Here was heroism evolved from pain and

R. B.                                                    E

disease.  Do you think the luxury of the Sybarites could breed that sort of thing? A Sybarite reared in luxury once visited a Spartan, and had to put up with Spartan simplicity and coarseness of food.  He said he thought the Spartans had been brave, but he knew them now to be the greatest cowards on earth, not to commit suicide rather than live so severely.  Mr. Browning holds that the fruit of all these victories stays and makes up for us the gain of life :—

> " I gather heart through just such conquests of the soul,
> Through evolution out of that which, on the whole,
> Was rough, ungainly, partial accomplishment, at best."

To have the fruit, we must have the root and stem and branch, and these must contend with the elements.  We must see—

> " By the means of Evil that Good is best,
> And, through earth and its noise, what is heaven's serene."

He sees another use for evil,—

> " Choose a joy !
> Bettered it was by sorrow gone before,
> And sobered somewhat by the shadowy sense
> Of sorrow which came after or might come.
> Joy, sorrow,—by precedence, subsequence—
> Either on each, make fusion, mix in Life
> That's both and neither wholly."

You know what a tonic work is. You know what becomes of muscles we do not exercise. Bind your arm to your side, you athlete, for two months; it will be withered when you unbind it. We get our great heroism by exercise. Mr. Browning says :—

> "For mankind springs
> Salvation by each hindrance interposed,
> They climb."

> " I can believe this dread machinery
> Of sin and sorrow, would confound me else,
> Devised, all pain, at most expenditure of pain,
> By who devised pain,—to evolve,
> By new machinery, in counterpart
> The moral qualities of man—
> To make him love and be beloved,
> Creating and self-sacrificing too,
> To enable man to wring, from out all pain,
> All pleasure for a common heritage."

By these things then man is compelled to strive, "which means, in man, as good as reach the goal."

So you see that Mr. Browning is what we call an optimist. Another article of his religion is belief in the immortality of the soul, because man is not here complete. Everything else is complete except man. Has man been developed

from the lower animals? The Poet does not
doubt it. Nevertheless he is now—

> "a man
> For aye removed from the developed brute,
> A god, though in the germ."

He is not complete yet; "man is not Man
as yet." His end, he says, is not attained while
only here and there a star shines out to dispel
the darkness, a Shakespeare here, a Milton
there, a Socrates and a Plato in one age, and a
Bacon and a Dante in other ages. The time
will come when God will make no more giants,
but elevate the race at once! Completion and
perfection are for star-fishes; you will never
see a better star-fish than you can pick up on
Brighton beach to-day.

> "Let the mere star-fish in his vault
>     Crawl in a wash of weed, indeed,
>     Rose-jacinth to the finger-tips;
> He, whole in body and soul, outstrips
> Man, found with either in default.
>     But what's whole, can increase no more."

> "Progress is man's distinctive mark alone,
>     Not God's and not the beast's. God is, they are,
>     Man partly is and wholly hopes to be."

Man has been and is so great that he sees

no prospect of his stopping in his development, and in his very greatness sees the promise of greater things to come.

> "I know this earth is not my sphere,
>   For I cannot so narrow me, but that
>   I still exceed it."

Remark that, in insisting upon the reasonableness of the immortality of the soul, Mr. Browning does not place it on the low orthodox ground which used to be held, that this life was nothing but a poor, wretched pilgrimage to something better. The waste, howling wilderness, the old hymn speaks of, where the only howling is made by the miserable, small-souled pilgrims themselves, finds no place in Mr. Browning's system. Boldly and clearly he speaks out on this point in the fine lines—

> "Another world!
> And why this world, this common world to be
> A make-shift, a mere foil how fair soever
> To some fine life to come?"

As a school, as a gymnasium, he will bate nothing of the value of this life; but a future life he thinks is indicated by man's longing for permanence, his manifest incompleteness here.

All through the poet's work, from first to

last, the belief in personal immortality, on reasonable grounds, is a main article of his creed. In this tabernacle life we were made to grow ; and the "broken arcs" of life demand something beyond, complementary to our poet's vision of the future. In all evil there is something remedial, something conservative in all suffering. There are worse things than having to live on sixpence a day and earning it. The great argument for immortality, is not for reward, but because it is *reasonable.* This life is far too short in which to do all we want. We only catch a few notes of the song, and it must be completed elsewhere. And this belief is not unscientific. It is the fashion to call it "unscientific." Physiology has not helped in the least iota to explain how it was that beef and beer made Hamlet's soliloquy. The atomic theory did not help us a bit ; therefore it is not unscientific to hold to a future life. With Browning it is a *hope*, neither more nor less, but still a hope.

This is a grand thing, coming from so great a genius of the Anglo-Saxon race—a man replete with the sciences and arts, and of profound learning and research. When such a man boldly said there is hope for a future life, it is a thing infinitely comforting to lesser souls who also looked forward with a little hope.

Now these reasonable beliefs are drawn, you will perceive, not from the Bible, not from the authority of the Christian or any other Church, but from the indications of a calm and liberal philosophy. Mr. Browning does not despise any man's creed or his no-creed; if it be honest and sincere, it is so far good. He has a wonderful poem termed *Christmas Eve.* A man goes into a miserable little Methodist chapel on Christmas Eve, and sits there till he falls asleep trying to listen to a vulgar sermon on the birth of Christ. As he sleeps he dreams of the various forms of Christianity. He fancies that he has left the chapel and gone out into the stormy night. And, lo! a great wonder happens to him : he thinks he sees in the splendour of the lunar rainbow the form of Christ, who has been present at that little chapel. The face of the Master turns towards him rather reproachfully, and in a moment he is caught up in His vesture and carried away to St. Peter's at Rome, there to behold another and a far grander form of worship on that same Christmas Eve. The Master enters, for amid all the mediævalism there was truth there also. There were the love and faith which had made Christian lands out of heathen lands, and softened the hard hearts of savage men. But faith and love were not all, and the Master wraps him in his mantle once more, to find intellect and know- ledge ; and soon they enter the lecture hall of a German university, where a professor is dis- coursing on the Christ-myth.

He refuses to enter here, but Christ goes within. There must then be truth here also, and so there is. The professor has pulverized the faith very, very fine indeed ; by his severe tests he has reduced the pearl of great price to ashes, "and yet in his judgment left it a pearl." He bids his followers treasure up the precious dust, by no means throw a particle away. Call it a .toy if they will ; it will serve a good purpose. There is something of value after all in the beautiful thing he has destroyed.

And so they leave the German professor, and the traveller is caught up again in the folds of the vesture of Christ, and he is taken back to the little chapel whence he started.

Ah! he says, he sees his error now ; he has despised the poor worship for its vulgarity. No longer, however, will he reject the water of life for sake of the coarseness of the vessel out of which he has to drink it.

I know no teaching which is more thoroughly healthful and wholesome than Browning's. There is none of that almost infernal, deadly resignation and insensibility to pain or pleasure which we see in Buddhist philosophy. He takes the pleasures and the ills of life as he finds them, and is cheerful and philosophical under all.

The God in which some find it so hard to believe is often but a caricature of God of which they have somehow got hold. We all believe in justice, mercy, and truth, which are the very fibres of God's being. These things to Browning spell *God.* He tells us " we must correct the portrait by the living face. Man's God, by God's God in the mind of man " (*The Pope,* p. 81).

We cannot expect to understand God, as his Bishop Blougram says :—

" Pure faith, indeed—you know not what you ask !
Naked belief in God the Omnipotent,

Omniscient, Omnipresent, sears too much
The sense of conscious creatures to be borne.
It were the seeing Him, no flesh shall dare.
Some think, creation's meant to show Him forth :
I say, it's meant to hide Him all it can ;
And that's what all the blessed evil's for.
Its use in time is to environ us,
Our breath, our drop of dew, with shield enough
Against that sight, till we can bear its stress.
Under a vertical sun, the exposed brain
And lidless eye and disimprisoned heart,
Less certainly would wither up at once,
Than mind confronted with the truth of Him.
But time and earth case-harden us to live ;
The feeblest sense is trusted most ; the child
Feels God a moment, ichors o'er the place,
Plays on, and grows to be a man like us."

He has written a very curious poem called
*The Epistle of Karshish*, supposed to be sent
by a doctor, who has heard the story of
Christ raising Lazarus from the dead. He
addresses his letter to his master in the science
of medicine, and speaks of Lazarus as doctors
talk to one another, calling it " a case." He
thinks he explains it by calling it one of
epilepsy, followed by a trance from which
Lazarus awoke, thinks Lazarus mad, but still
is wonderfully puzzled by all he has told him,
and then breaks out into this fine appeal :—

> " The very God ! think, Abib ;
>     Dost thou think ?
>   So, the All-Great, were the All-Loving too—
>   The Madman saith He said so ; it is strange."

He believes in the gospel of work ; he recognises with true scientific perception that
cessation of use means degeneration, atrophy,
loss. The correlation between work and food
is so intimate, that we cannot say which Nature
values more highly. The apostle said, "If a man
will not work, neither shall he eat." Nature
seems to say, If he will not work, he shall not
exist at all ; certainly not without retrogression
to the most degraded of types.

Browning says :—

> " And so I live, you see,
>   Go through the world, try, prove, reject,
>   Prefer, still struggling to effect
>   My warfare ; happy that I can
>   Be crossed and thwarted as a man,
>   Not left in God's contempt apart,
>   With ghastly smooth life, dead at heart,
>   Tame in earth's paddock as her prize "
>
> .     .     .     .

And again,—

> " Learning anew the use of soldiership,
>   Self-abnegation, freedom from all fear,
>   Loyalty to the life's end ! Ruminate,

Deserve the initiatory spasm,—once more
Work, be unhappy but bear life, my son!"
*Ring and Book*, vol. iv., p. 53.

Be faithful, says our Mr. Greatheart :—

"Thus at first prompting of what I call God,
And fools call Nature, didst hear, comprehend,
Accept the obligation laid on thee

.        .        .        .

As brute and bird do, reptile and the fly,
Ay and, I nothing doubt, even tree, shrub, plant
And flower o' the field, all in a common pact
To worthily defend the trust of trusts,
Life from the Ever Living."
*Ring and Book*, vol. iv., p. 47.

No whining about life not being worth living here, because of the inevitable trials we must encounter.   No!

"For mankind springs salvation by each hindrance inter-
posed."
*Sordello*, p. 195.

"Do something," says Carlyle, in the same strain :—

" Be no longer a chaos, but a World, or even a Worldkin, Produce ! Produce ! Were it but the pitifullest infinitesimal fraction of a product, produce it, in God's name!"

He does not say, with Tennyson :—

" Oh yet we trust that *somehow* good
   Will be the final goal of ill,
   To pangs of nature, sins of will,
Defects of doubt, and taints of blood ;

That nothing walks with aimless feet ;
   That not one life shall be destroy'd,
   Or cast as rubbish to the void,
When God hath made the pile complete."

No ; beautiful as this faith is, Browning's is stronger and his vision clearer. With him is no *somehow ;* but he shows us just how the ill tends to good, and we have not to wait till the pile is completed ; but we see the Builder at work, putting into His fabric the unlikely looking " rubbish " we too rashly thought would be cast aside.

I say, with all deference to those who know Mr. Browning's works better than I do, that it appears to me we cannot properly understand them till we clearly recognise what is the poet's " Estimate of Life." I think that estimate is *unique*, that it is eminently *scientific*, and that it is pre-eminently *good* for us to recognise. I should say that the theme, as musicians call it, of all our poet's work is—*that no factors in our life* (however unpromising they may appear) *can be spared consistently with our development and progress.*

He does not complain with Dryden, that "Life is all a cheat," nor ask plaintively with Gay, "Oh, what is life with ills encompassed round?" He laments not with Shakespeare that "Life's but a walking shadow—a tale told by an idiot, full of sound and fury signifying nothing"; nor with that other who said, "Life is a weary interlude that leaves no epilogue but death"; nor with him who grieved, "The longer life, the greater choice of evil." He calls it not "a mist," "a riddle," "a shadow," "a wind-swept meadow." Nothing of all this in Browning; with him, as in *Fra Lippo,*—

"The world and life's too big to pass for a dream."

As in *Saul,*—

"How good is man's life, the mere living! how fit to employ
All the heart and the soul and the senses for ever in joy!"

"I have lived, seen God's hand thro' a lifetime, and all was for best!"

As in *Rabbi Ben Ezra,*—

"Perfect I call Thy plan;
Thanks that I was a man;"

As once more in *Fra Lippo Lippi,*—

> "This world's no blot for us
> Nor blank ; it means intensely, and means good."

And as again in *The Guardian Angel,*—

> "O world, as God has made it! All is beauty :
> And knowing this is love, and love is duty."

He goes to the Morgue, and even there, contemplating the corpses of the poor wretches on the slabs, can exclaim with his beautiful, healthy optimism,—

> "My own hope is, a sun will pierce
> The thickest cloud earth ever stretched ;
> That, after Last, returns the First,
> Though a wide compass round be fetched ;
> That what began best can't end worst,
> Nor what God blessed once prove accurst."

And in that magnificent *Abt Vogler* poem,—

> "There shall never be one lost good! What was shall
> live as before ;
> The evil is null, is nought, is silence implying sound ;
> What was good, shall be good, with, for evil, so much
> good more ;
> On the earth the broken arcs ; in the heaven, a perfect
> round."

The *In Memoriam* utterances sound like

the voice of Mr. Little-Faith, after listening to
such a defiance of evil as this.

From *Pauline* (Mr. Browning's first poem,
written, I may add, for the benefit of those who
may not know the order of his works, in 1832,
when he was but twenty), where he says :—

> " Feeling God loves us, and that all that errs
> Is a strange dream which death will dissipate "—

through the splendid triumphs of his genius—
*Paracelsus, Sordello, Men and Women, Fifine,*
down to his last work, we have the same un-
diminished, nay, accentuated, confidence that
" the soul, stung to strength through weakness,
strives for good through evil," because " Law
deals the same with soul and body "; and I say
that such a long life of consistent facing the
ills of time, with confidence that " God's in His
heaven, all's right with the world "—while the
limp, degenerate jelly-fish who prate about life
not being worth living, and, because they are
emasculate and jaundiced, dare to tell us, with
their poisoned melancholy, that life is a long
mistake—entitles Mr. Browning to a perfectly
unique position among the prophets of our day :
and because I believe him to occupy this place

in literature, I have taken leave to term him a scientific poet, a thesis I am still prepared to maintain. And for this reason, that he recognises the great Darwinian truth that opposition and struggle are the great factors in development and progress ; that as with the organs of animals and plants, which are the outcome of their necessity, so with our souls, in the words of Dewey : " Human virtue is the result of effort and patience in the circumstances that most directly try it. All wisdom and worth in the world are a struggle with ignorance, infirmity, and temptation ; there is not an admirable character presented before you but it has cost years and years of toil, and watching, and self-government to form it." The struggles of orchids to secure cross fertilization have evolved their rich, beautiful forms ; and our own struggle after good serves to evolve our noblest faculties.

> " Our business with the sea
> Is not with air, but o' the water, watery :
> We must endure the false, no particle of which
> Do we acquaint us with, but up we mount a pitch
> Above it, find our head reach truth, while hands explore
> The false below."
> *Fifine at the Fair.*

R. B.                                         F

He despises not the grosser element; "he moves in it, yet resists; is upborne on every side by what he beats against"; "The prize is in the process."

This doctrine runs through all his work as a vein of gold, not merely shining here and there, but running as a clue to his teaching throughout; and if this is not in the methods of science, so much the worse for science.

Then again, the true scientific mind never loses sight of the smallest fact which can throw any light on the subject of investigation. Mr. Browning is remarkable for never ignoring the apparently insignificant factors in the life-history of his characters. He deals with the whole of these factors, not with a part only, as do so many writers. He must have everything before he will construct his parallelogram of forces.

> "Oh, the little more, and how much it is !
> And the little less, and what worlds away ! "
> *By the Fireside.*

Now it is a scientific truism, that it is the little overlooked forces ever at work which are always changing the face of our world. The present age has learned to write the epic of the worm ; we are beginning to duly estimate the value of the infinitely little. And not less true is it that our mental development depends on a number of circumstances which we are too apt to overlook. It has recently been discovered that Mr. Darwin, careful as he always seemed in allowing for the fullest importance of minutest causes, made a great mistake in his account of the origin of the coral reefs in the Pacific; it has been urged that he did not make nearly sufficient allowance for the effects of those trifling causes, and attributed the origin of these coral islands to forces which it has been shown have had much less to do with them than he supposed—the fact being that apparently the most unlikely things had far the most work to do.*

So is it with our own lives and characters ; it is the unceasing play of mean and paltry things which mould them. Browning is always insisting on the value of these trifles. We neither become angels nor devils all at once.

---

* This was written before Mr. Huxley's reply to the Duke of Argyll in the *Nineteenth Century* appeared. Whether Darwin was right or wrong has not yet been decided, but the illustration will still serve.

Our poet is always taking us behind the scenes and showing us his characters preparing for the parts they play. He points out just where the paint and the padding come in. He is as merciless with his heroes and heroines as the valet to his master; but that is because he knows them as intimately.

Now all this is healthy and pre-eminently useful, as we said at the outset. It is well to know that "the laughing loves" at the base of the cup are not more valued in the Master's eye than "the skull things in order grim" about its rim. We are not to look "down but up! to uses of a cup."

> "What I aspired to be,
> And was not, comforts me:"

"'Tis not what man Does, but what man Would do, which exalts him."

Though we cannot bring the sum right, Browning always gives us credit for the working. He judges never by the world's standard of success or failure, and is always putting down the mighty from their seats and exalting the humble and the meek.

Do we succeed? It is due to "just this or

that poor impulse, which for once had play unstifled."—*Cristina.*

Do we fail ? though we tried so hard—

> " That low man seeks a little thing to do,
>     Sees it and does it :
> This high man, with a great thing to pursue,
>     Dies ere he knows it.
>
> That low man goes on adding one to one,
>     His hundred's soon hit :
> This high man, aiming at a million,
>     Misses an unit.
> That, has the world here—should he need the next,
>     Let the world mind him !
> This, throws himself on God, and unperplexed
>     Seeking shall find him."
>
> A Grammarian's Funeral.

> " Better have failed in the high aim, as I,
>     Than vulgarly in the low aim succeed
> As, God be thanked, I do not ! "
>
> The Inn Album.

> " There is Heaven, since there is Heaven's simulation—
>     Earth :
> I sit possessed in patience : prison roof
> Shall break one day and Heaven beam overhead."

All this sympathy with failure is so helpful to the poor handicapped ones who are always being pushed aside in life's race. I shall be told, I suppose, that this proves Browning to be unscientific—that the survival of the fittest theory does not provide for the failures.

> " A tree born to erectness of bole,
> Palm or plane or pine, we laud if lofty, columnar—
> Little if athwart, askew,—leave to the axe and the flame !
> Where is the vision may penetrate earth and beholding
>     acknowledge
> Just one pebble at root ruined the straightness of stem ?
> Whose fine vigilance follows the sapling, accounts for the
>     failure,—
> Here blew wind, so it bent : there the snow lodged, so it
>     broke ? "
>
> *Ixion.*

But the whole business of modern science is just now devoted to getting rid of the pebbles at our roots and propping up our weakly boles. The failures were never so well looked after as now. For though " all's Law, yet all's Love " too, thank God. We have said little of Love in all this argument, not because there is little of it in Browning; it is the dominant note of his work—

> " As some imperial chord subsists,
> Steadily underlies the accidental mists
> Of music springing thence, that run their mazy race
> Around."
>
> *Fifine.*

# BROWNING AS A SCIENTIFIC POET.

THE commonly accepted notion of poets and poetry excludes the idea of the scientific habit of thought, and still more of its expression. We expect the poet to speak to us, in metrical language, of the passions and interests of man, and to interpret for us the voice of nature in strains that are not hampered by exactitude and precision. In other words, we grant him "the poet's licence." But as all this is just the opposite to our demands on the man of science, it seems a contradiction in terms to speak of a scientific poet. It jars upon our ideas of the fitness of things. But why? Because they are conventional ideas; and our notions of poets and what constitutes true poetry, are not always inspired by familiarity with the greatest masters of the art. The scientific method, it is true, is not in favour with the minor poets; and it is not given even to all the greater to combine with the highest poetic faculty the deeper insight into the hidden things of nature possessed by

Robert Browning. In him, as I hope to show, the poetic and scientific methods are not merely found together, but are truly combined; and throughout his works are scattered abundant evidence that he, with keen vision, has seen far into the workings of Nature, and ennobled his phrase and verse from the study of her phenomena.

Milton has done this too; and Tennyson has proved that the scientific spirit can enrich his verse, and that he, in turn, can invest the operations of natural laws with the enchantment of his art. Who could have imagined that a poet would have stated the atomic theory of Lucretius in the magnificent terms that he has done ?—

> "A void was made in Nature; all her bonds
> Cracked; and I saw the flaring atom-streams
> And torrents of her myriad universe,
> Ruining along the illimitable inane,
> Fly on, to clash together again, and make
> Another and another frame of things
> For ever."

As a specimen of Tennyson's poetry, I don't think any one can say it is spoiled by being a statement, and an accurate one, of the atomic theory.

And if for Browning it be true that—

> "Verse was a temple-worship vague and vast,
> A ceremony that withdrew the last
> Opposing bolt, looped back the lingering veil
> Which hid the holy place,"
>
> *(Pauline,)*

what wonder if he speak of the deepest things the holy place enshrines in the sacred language that befits its service ?

It would probably not add to Mr. Browning's popularity were the world convinced of his advanced standpoint. It is not apt to love overmuch to be taken out of its depth ; it likes its poets to sing as caged birds are taught to warble—songs piped by itself, and demands of its Sordellos that they shall be bards and not philosophers :

> "Why introduce crotchets like these? fine surely, but no use
> In poetry—which still must be, to strike,
> Based upon common sense ; there's nothing like
> Appealing to our nature.
>
> .     .     .     .     .     .     .
>
> .Would you have your songs endure ?
> Build on the human heart."
>
> *Sordello.*

Apart from the fact that we are not accustomed to find the poetic and scientific natures co-exist, there seems a tacit understanding that it is somehow an offence (even when they do) if the poet trench on the other's province.    In a humorous letter to the *Pall Mall Gazette* the other day, on the question whether a certain flower of delicious odour should be called "tube-rose" or "tuber-rose," the writer says that he is "deeply distressed to hear that *tube-rose* is so called from its being a 'lumpy flower.' It is not at all lumpy, and even if it were, no poet should be heartless enough to say so.    Henceforth there really must be two derivations for every word, one for the poet, and one for the scientist.    And in the present case the poet will dwell on the tiny trumpets of ivory into which the white flower breaks, and leave to the man of science horrid allusions to its supposed lumpiness, and indiscreet revelations of its private life below ground.    In fact, tuber as a derivation is disgraceful.    On the roots of verbs philology may be allowed to speak, but on the roots of flowers she must keep silence.    We cannot allow her to dig up Parnassus."

Darwin's investigations into the fertilization of plants, and the part which their colours and

forms play in that process, must have been felt by
poets of the lower school as almost an outrage;
yet to a Browning these discoveries serve only
to awaken ideas and set up trains of thought of
infinitely more value,—as being in harmony with
the spirit of nature,—than they could have ever
imagined who only thought of the redness of
the rose and the blueness of the violet as ad-
juncts with the graces of their form to make the
fields and woods look pretty.

He is in sympathy with those who can tell us
what is the hidden meaning of the "objects
that throng our youth." "We see and hear,
and do not wonder much."

> "As German Bœhme never cared for plants
> Until it happed, a-walking in the fields,
> He noticed all at once that plants could speak,
> Nay, turned with loosened tongue to talk with him.
> That day the daisy had an eye indeed—
> Colloquized with the cowslip on such themes!"
>
> *Poems,* vol. v., p. 208.

It is not demanded of the poet that he
should ignore the beauty of the rainbow till he
has studied Fraunhofer's lines. What we do
say is, that neither the scientist alone nor the
poet alone comprehend Nature till they borrow
from each other—the one the reverence and

the worship, the other the learning and loving study, that, united, make up the true spirit in which she is to be approached. In Robert Browning there is the happiest combination of these requisites.

He has learned with delight how the human brain enshrines its mysteries in its myriad cells, where thought is born and memory treasures her precious records; of the marvellous mechanism of our limbs, with their cords and pulleys, and facile play; of the eye, that with insatiable activity supplies the brain with its impressions of the world around us; of the musical instrument of ten thousand strings, played on by the air-pulsations that arouse the sense of hearing to activity every moment of our waking lives.

In a very beautiful passage in *Ferishtah* (p. 76) he makes the Creator address man thus—

> "Wherefore did I contrive for thee that ear
> Hungry for music, and direct thine eye
> To where I hold a seven-stringed instrument,
> Unless I meant thee to beseech Me play?"

Here, of course, the reference is to the organ of Corti in the internal ear, with its 3,000 arches, its keys ranged like those of a piano, aptly described by the poet as " hungry for music." The seven-stringed instrument, I need not say, is light and the seven colours of the spectrum.

It is nothing wonderful that he should know such easily-acquired facts ; it *is* wonderful that they should be transfigured by the magic of his art. Yet he imparts his secret to the attentive reader. It is his deep love of the law and harmony of nature. His process has been that which Henry Taylor describes as his own : " Observation of facts ; generalization from facts observed ; rejection into the concrete, but with improvements from the fancy, of the general conclusions obtained."

The more thoroughly the lover of Nature is skilled in the knowledge of her laws, the greater will be the intellectual pleasure with which he will contemplate them ; and the poet who can follow Nature into her secret chambers, and commune with her on her deepest phenomena, will be the poet who has the noblest things to say to the human soul. The poet who can interpret for us the " great symphony of organic harmony composed in the forest key," as Mr.

Mivart terms it, speaking of the vegetable world of the Brazils—of the recently-discovered harmonious relations of the ocean and its submerged wealth of wondrous beauty, will be the poet of the future who will come into a closer relationship with man than has ever been reached before. So far from the fascination of Nature being dispelled by our completer knowledge of her laws, it has been a hundredfold increased by the revelation of glories before undreamed of, which are none the less resplendent because we know their origin. How science and poetry can blend in one harmonious spirit, students of Henry Thoreau need not be told.

By science in this connection I do not mean merely mental science, without which a poet could not hope " to loop back the veil." We know how versed in this was Shakespeare. Coleridge speaks of "Shakespeare's deep and accurate science in mental philosophy." No one will deny, I presume, this characteristic to Robert Browning; but I claim something more than this for him. I maintain that in his works he exhibits a deep and earnest sympathy with all branches of human knowledge dealing with

the causes and connections of natural phenomena—in other words, with what we term the
physical sciences. Now this is essentially an
age pre-eminent for the investigation of such
causes and connections; yet I think we may
say that in its atmosphere there is nothing that
need stunt and dwarf the spirit of poetry. I do
not quite see with Mr. Radford, in his remarks
on Mr. Bury's paper, "that the language of
poetry and science are diametrically opposed."
They need not use the same language of course;
but I can see no reason for opposition between
the spirit of poetry and that of science. Poetry
and the physical sciences flourished together in
the Greek intellect; and though perhaps, as far
as modern times are concerned, till the advent
of Haller and Goethe, the scientific and the
poetic minds had not been blended, we have in
Goethe a grand example of the genus; and in
Browning, as I think, we have the noble forerunner of a new, strong race of poets of the
first order, the interpreters of the inquiring,
analytical soul of the age, in which no subject
is too sacred to be questioned. No; were the
physical sciences, like our factory chimneys, to
exhale a breath poisonous to the surrounding

flora of the poet's fancy, as some have thought,
we should be terrible losers by all our advance-
ment in the productive arts, and Mr. Ruskin's
lament over our decadence be more than
justified.  The spirit of the age has dissolved
the legend of William Tell, and taken some of
the romance out of the Tell country ; but it has
given it a magnificent railway, which in a few
hours brings the flowers and fruits of Italy to
cheerless London slums.

The poet of the future will see more romance
in that fact than in many time-honoured legends.
He will have to sing to us of the modern Spirit
of the Alps—Professor Tyndall, in his chalet,
questioning the rainbow, the glacier, the ava-
lanche, and the mountain mist and storm.  The
dragons are gone, and the knights that slew
them live only in legendary tales ; but the
epidemiologist, in his laboratory, doing battle
with the germs of cholera and typhus, is a not
less noble theme for the poet of the nineteenth
century, though an artist might not think the
subject would look so well on his canvas.  It
was a poet, Lucretius, who eighteen hundred
years ago anticipated the atomic theory.  We
owe him a debt of gratitude for proving in his

own person that poetry is not incompatible with science, and that it is quite possible for a man to investigate the laws of nature without blinding his vision to the loveliness of the ideal world. He sang the reign of law in the universe, that our misery or our happiness was not dependent on the caprice of the gods, but on the nature of things. This man was the true poet, *the creator;* and it has taken the world eighteen centuries to prove as facts what his prophetic spirit foresaw. We live now in an age of technical accuracy. The time of the poet's licence is past; and poetry, if not now scientifically accurate, is to us of this age foolishness. Some one has said that a poet who was not mad was no poet at all. If Mr. Browning has any madness, it is in his method, never in his matter. His is emphatically the sound mind in the sound body; he is the poet of downright common sense; his imagination never runs away with him, though possibly it is exhausted in his style. Scientific students of Browning must often think what a scientist he would have made, just as readers of Professor Tyndall are always exclaiming, " Here is the poet of science!" Hear what he himself

R. B. G

says of the experimental philosopher : " He lives a life of the senses, using his hands, eyes, and ears in his experiments, but is constantly being carried beyond the margin of the senses. His mind must realize the subsensible world, and possess a pictorial power ; if the picture so formed be correct, the phenomena he is investigating are accounted for.   Imagination with him does not sever itself from the world of fact; this is the storehouse from which all its pictures are drawn ; and the magic of its art consists, not in creating things anew, but in so changing the magnitude, position, and other relations of sensible things as to fit them for the requirements of the intellect in the sub-sensible world."   Poets have been allowed to exercise a riotous power in dealing capriciously with facts.   But if a well-ordered and disciplined scientific method restrain this riot and caprice, I don't think the result is any the less true poetry.   Perhaps the fact that Browning is restrained by his science from playing havoc with phenomena may account for the *un*re-strained riot and caprice of his words.   On Tyndall's theory this may really be Browning's safety-valve.

Christopher North and the Ettrick Shepherd in the twenty-second of the *Noctes Ambrosianæ* so exactly and admirably place the question in its proper light, that I may be pardoned if I quote a few sentences.

The Shepherd asks, "What think ye, sir, o' the dogma, that high imagination is incompatible wi' high intellect, and that as science flourishes poetry decays ? "

North replies, "The dogmata of dunces are beyond the reach of redemption. A man may have a high intellect with little or no imagination ; but he cannot have a high imagination with little or no intellect. The intellect of Homer, Dante, Milton, or Shakespeare, was higher than that of Aristotle, Newton, and Bacon. When elevated by feeling into imagination, their intellect becomes transcendent, and thus were they poets, the noblest name by far and away that belongs to any of the children of men.' What is science? True knowledge of mind and matter, as far as it is permitted to us to know anything truly of the world without and the world within us, congenial in their co-existence. What is poetry ? The true exhibition in musical and metrical speech

of the thoughts of humanity when coloured by
its feelings throughout the whole range of the
physical, moral, intellectual, and spiritual regions
of its being.   Poetry and science are identical
—or rather, that as imagination is the highest
kind of intellect, so poetry is the highest kind
of science.   It is only in an age of science that
anything worthy the name of poetry can exist.
In a rude age there may be bursts of passion—
of imagination even, which, if you insist on
calling them poetry, I am willing so to designate ; in that case, almost all human language
is poetry.   Will any antiquary or archæologist
show me a bit of poetry as broad as the palm
of my hand worth the toss up of a tinker's
farthing the produce of uncivilized man ?   Not
till man and nature and human life lie in the
last light of science—that is, of knowledge and
of truth—will poetry reach the acme of its
triumph.   As Campbell sings,—

> " ' Come, bright Improvement, on the car of Time,
> And rule the spacious world from clime to clime,'—

and still poetry will be here below Prime
Minister and High Priest of Nature."
People say that when we have solved all the

mysteries of Nature, the sentiment will be all gone and poetry die out, and therefore the phrase "scientific poet" is a contradiction in terms. The cynical philosopher who, when his wife cried for the first time in his presence with the hope of softening his heart in the direction of a milliner's bill, assured her that tears would not move him in the least, as he knew their exact constituents, and was not going to waste his money on account of an exhibition of a solution of phosphate and muriate of soda—though probably a good chemist had not enough intellect to raise him to poetry; and there is no reason to suppose that the knowledge that lightning is electricity will destroy the grandeur of an Alpine storm, or that cloud-forms, the play of light and colour on a mountain side, or the dew-drops on a leaf, will cease to be poetical because their causes are well understood. The tear-drops in the eye of a beautiful woman will surely not be less beautiful because we are "familiarly acquainted with the perfected philosophy of all secretions."

Now it is because, from a careful study of Mr. Browning's works, I have come to the

conclusion that the poet is intimately acquainted
with the physical sciences, that I hold him to
be for this very reason so much the more a
great poet—the greatest living poet; he can
touch us the closer because he knows more
about us than we know ourselves, more about·
our environments, more about the phenomena
that encircle our lives.   We yield ourselves up
to him; our secret thoughts are not hid from
him; he knows our anatomy to the backbone.
It is his character of all-roundness that makes
him excel.   He knows everything; if we
can't understand him, it is because we know
so much less than he.   He is always right.
Often he appears unintelligible.   One ransacks
dictionaries and encyclopædias; it is they that
are defective, not Browning wanting.   And
all this amazing wealth of learning sits so easily
on him that he wears it as if he had been born
in it, and, to me, at least, he never appears
pedantic.   Are you a lawyer? he talks to you
as if he had been all his life in the long robe;
a physician? you never had a professor of
medicine so close at your heart as Paracelsus;
a theologian? he has all the wisdom of the
Schoolmen and the love of John himself; and

so with all his students he is in closer touch than any other poet since Shakespeare the divine. The artist loves him as a brother of the pencil, the musician claims him of his kin, and the scientist, opening his works where he will, sees in every line intimations that here is the master of all others who can hold council with him on equal terms, and finds in him a brother to rejoice with him and "triumph o'er each secret wrung from Nature's cold reserve." This is an immense claim to make, but it can be sustained; and its very immensity serves to explain the slow but steady progress our poet has made past all lower niches towards the highest seats where the gods are.

Carlyle demanded of a truly great man that he must be all sorts of men, and had little respect for "poets who could only sit on chairs and compose stanzas"—Browning must have gone to his heart. Not in the sense satirized in "the Loves of the triangles" or "the Loves of the plants" is our poet all this to us, but in the fact that he has so largely imbibed and assimilated the science of the time that almost every page of his works is permeated by its influence. Sometimes this is shown by a word

or two that passes unnoticed by a reader who
is not familiar with the ideas the word calls
up, as, for instance, in the lines :—

" The child feels God a moment,
    Ichors o'er the place, plays on, and grows to be a man
    like us."

In the expression " ichors o'er the place "
is found a beautiful illustration from the physiology of repair in injured skin surfaces and
the pathology of wounds.    As the cicatrix
closes up the cut flesh, so does the child's mind
become case-hardened after the first effects of
the awfulness of the Infinite One's apprehended
presence have passed away.    The time soon
comes when " God is not in all his thoughts."

In some cases we have an actual statement
of a scientific truth in so many words, as in
*Sordello* :—

" A soul—above his soul
    Power to uplift his power,—this moon's control
    Over the sea depths."                    P. 187.

And again :—

" Wherefore doubt
    That love meet for such strength, some moon without
    Would match his sea ? "

                                        P. 189.

Sometimes he is actually technical, as in some lines of *Prince Hohenstiel Schwangau* (p. 45) :—

> "Try to make good do good as evil does—
> Were just as if a chemist, wanting white,
> And knowing black ingredients bred the dye,
> Insisted these too should be white forsooth."

His optimism is always cropping up ; and it is not surprising he should cull illustrations from chemistry, which abounds in examples of good and beautiful things produced from worthless and ugly substances. The lovely series of aniline dyes made from coal tar, for instance, might surely afford a scientific poet of an optimistic turn of mind some help in this direction. In the lines just quoted the idea, that to get the highest good we must have some evil amongst the ingredients, is not elaborated ; but those who are only slightly acquainted with chemical manipulations will not want more than the poet's hint to see the force of his theory.

He states the same truth in another form in *Pietro* :—

> "Fair and good are products—of Foul and Evil : one
> must bring to pass the other.

> Just as poisons grow drugs, steal through sundry odd
>    ducts
> Doctors name, and ultimately issue safe and changed.
> You'd abolish poisons, treat disease with dainties
> Such as suit the sound and sane?   With all such kick-
>    shaws vain you pother !
> Arsenic 's the stuff puts force into the faint eyes,
> Opium sets the brain to rights—by cark and care de-
>    ranged."

In that sublime poem *Easter Day* (p. 191)
there is a very remarkable instance of Mr.
Browning's way of wrapping up a great
scientific truth in two or three words, and
leaving it without recurring to it, or drawing
attention to the force of the illustration by
elaboration of the idea.   Browning never beats
his nuggets into leaf—it is rather in its very
concentration that his force exists.

> " Thy choice was earth : thou didst attest
> 'Twas fitter spirit should subserve
> The flesh, than flesh refine to nerve
> Beneath the spirit's play."

How many thousands of readers have passed
over these most remarkable lines and missed
all their force and beauty, because, unlike the
author of them, who seems to have a perfectly

voracious appetite for facts, they did not know they contained a precise statement of the origin of the nervous system according to our greatest physiologists. *Easter Day* was, I think, written in Florence in 1850. I believe it was not till 1855 that Herbert Spencer · published his *Principles of Psychology*, and therein speculated on the evolution of the first rudiments of a nervous system in Medusæ and other low types of animal life ; his speculations having since to some extent been confirmed by the investigations of Romanes and Eimer. Herbert Spencer points out how an impression or stimulus comes to habitually traverse a certain path along the lines of least resistance, thus leading to a differentiation of the protoplasm. Bastian, in his *Brain as an Organ of the Mind* (p. 21), says, " Wherever external impressions produce molecular movements which traverse with frequency some definite path, the transference of such movements is made easier by each repetition, and there is a tendency to the initiation of a structural change along this path. Ultimately by the constant repetition of such a process we should have the gradual formation of an actual ' Nerve fibre.' "

Now I know of no writer anterior to Mr. Spencer who suggested this as the process by which nerves are formed ; yet Mr. Browning— in a highly concentrated manner it is true, but still actually—seems to have anticipated the great and interesting discovery.

In *Numpholeptos* (p. 97) these lines occur :—

> " As flash may find
> The inert nerve, sting awake the palsied limb."

The reference is to the use made of electricity in medical science, and the fact that by its aid a paralysed muscle can be restored to its normal condition. No reader of Browning can have failed to remark how great an accumulator of facts he is—facts of all sorts, and from every conceivable and out-of-the-way place. Odd scraps of lore here and there on every possible subject demonstrate that nothing in the range of human learning is beneath his notice or un-worthy of being treasured in his storehouse ; this is essentially the scientific habit of mind, and this habit has largely contributed to his greatness. Voltaire said, " There can be no great poetry without great wisdom," and Horace had said it before him. Although it is true enough that the poet is born and not made, it is equally true, as Carpenter says, "that the imaginative faculty may be directed and invigorated, cultivated and chastened by volitional effort." Mr. Browning's industry it is that makes him so difficult to the careless reader.

If at times he is unintelligible, it is because he knows so much more than we do. The automatic action of our faculties is in direct proportion to their exercise; and it is because Browning has travelled over so vast a range of subjects, getting at the soul of all things, and analysing the deepest things of man, that he has become to us the seer and the sayer of the abysmal things of life and their awfullest mysteries. He knew what was required of him. "A poet must be earth's essential king," he declares. He who aspires to the poet's crown needs everything. "Red, green, and blue that whirl into a white, the variance now, the essential unity which makes the miracle." And this reminds me that Browning makes very great use throughout his work of similes derived from his study of light. Here are a few :—

" Rather learn and love each facet flash of the revolving
    year !
Red, green, and blue that whirl into a white."
                            *Ring and Book*, vol. i. p. 71.

" Only the prism's obstruction shows aright
The secret of a sunbeam, breaks its light
Into the jewelled bow from blankest white ;
So may a glory from defect arise ! "
                            *Poems*, vol. vi. p. 151.

Again—

" Light, thwarted, breaks
A limpid purity to rainbow flakes."
                            *Sordello*, p. 170.

Self-sacrifice he terms losing " the varicolour
in achromatic white."—*Fifine*, p. 65.

The singularly beautiful poem *Nympholeptos*
owes its remarkable imagery to the figure of
light rays decomposed by gems, the perfect
white of the diamond sending forth prismatic
colours, and these again traced back to their
source leading to the pure cold moonbeam.
So the pure white silver light of the loved one
rays forth blood-streaks, sun warmth, sun light,
and salvation.

" Warms the soul, it sweetens, softens.
' What fairy track do I explore ?
What magic hall return to, like the gem,
Centuply angled o'er a diadem ?    ·         ·

You dwell there, hearted ; from your midmost home
Rays forth—through that fantastic world I roam
Ever—from centre to circumference,
Shaft upon coloured shaft,' this crimsons thence,
That purples out its præcinct through the waste.
Surely I had your sanction what I faced,
Fared forth upon that untried yellow ray,
Whence I retrack my steps ?

     .     .     .     .     .

Irradiation, late triumphant through the distance finds its fate
Merged in your pure blank soul, alike the source and
    tomb of that prismatic glow."
                    *Numpholeptos*, p. 101.

As a commentary on this suggestive poem, consider the influence the study of the life and character of the Virgin Mary has had on the minds of millions of men and women. The pure moonbeam of her smile has proved to this a path of gold, "for gold means love," to another many a daring crimson, blood-red path of passionate devotion, such as filled that Spanish knight of Isabella's who braved the fury of the Moor, and wrote Our Lady's name over the portals of the mosque at Granada. To how many others a violet path of humble service and devotion ! A pure ideal, once dowered to the world, has never merely rested in its gem-like, faceted beauty, but has brought forth bright and glorious paths of colour that have filled our souls with every kind of grace and loveliness. The conception of the idea of Our Lady, though it were founded in no historic basis of fact, has done the work of the faceted gem to beautify all that came within the scope of its glory. We owe this exquisite illustration to Browning's study of decomposed rays of light, and their recomposition into complete or white light.

In Professor Tyndall's address on the Scientific Limit of the Imagination he tells us that " two-thirds of the rays emitted by the sun fail to arouse in the eye the sense of vision. The rays exist, but the visual organ requisite for their translation into light does not exist. And so, from this region of darkness and mystery which surrounds us, rays may now be darting which require but the development of the proper intellectual organs to translate them into knowledge as far surpassing ours as ours surpasses that of the wallowing reptiles which once held possession of this planet."

Mr. Browning, in *Jochanan Hakkadosh* states the same truth in other words, words that

I think we shall understand all the better after those of Professor Tyndall :—

> " O Thou Almighty who canst re-instate
> Truths in their primal clarity, confused
> By man's perception, which is man's and made
> To suit his service,—how, once disabused
> Of reason which sees light half shine half shade,
> Because of flesh, the medium that adjusts
> Purity to his visuals, both an aid
> And hindrance,—how to eyes earth's air encrusts,
> When purged and perfect to receive truth's beam
> Pouring itself on the new sense it trusts
> With all its plenitude of power,—how seem
> Then, the intricacies of shade, of shine,
> Oppugnant natures—Right and Wrong, we deem
> Irreconcilable?   O eyes of mine,
> Freed now of imperfection, ye avail
> To see the whole sight."

Embryologists tell us that man, in his development in the embryo, passes through the various stages of fish, reptile, bird, and mammiferous quadruped, till it ultimately arrives at the human stage. Hugh Miller remarks the same thing of the development of the human brain ; in succession we have the brain of the inferior natures till the unique character of the human brain is assumed. And if we carefully study the origin of mind in the lower animals we shall find there is scarcely an attribute pos-

R. B.                                     H

sessed by man, scarcely a virtue or faculty that, in a more or less crude and undeveloped form, is not found in the creatures beneath us. We open our Browning and find he knows all about it. It is not new to him that "man is the sum total of all the animals."

In *Paracelsus* (p. 189), he says there are :—

> "Imperfect qualities throughout creation
> Suggesting some one creature yet to make,
> Some point where all those scattered rays should meet
> Convergent in the faculties of man.
>
> .        .        .        .        .
>
> Hints and previsions of which faculties
> Are strewn confusedly everywhere about
> The inferior natures, and all lead up higher,
> All shape out dimly the superior race,
> The heir of hopes too fair to turn out false,
> And man appears at last."

And just as inferior brains and natures point to the advent of man, so did the early brain and nature of primeval man foreshadow the higher and nobler man, and so do now the powers and potentialities of our highest races point on, ever forward, to the man that is to be—

> "Progress is the law of life, man is not Man as yet."
> "But in completed man begins anew
> A tendency to God."   "For God is glorified in man."
>
> *Paracelsus,* pp. 190, 191.

If there be any who hold that "man is Nature's crowning blunder," our poet is not of their number.

From Browning's earliest to his latest work we may gather hundreds of examples such as we have quoted, to show how deeply science has tinctured his thought and how heartily he is imbubed with its love. In *Pauline*, which in one sense is a prelude to *Paracelsus*, he again and again recurs to the theme so grandly elaborated in the latter work of the consecration of a soul to knowledge, one in whom was—

> "A principle of restlessness
> Which would be all, have, see, know, taste, feel, all."

> "This restlessness of passion meets in me
> A craving after knowledge."

As in *Paracelsus*, so in *Pauline*, the lesson for us is, knowledge must never be pursued at the expense of love.

With Browning it is ever love first, all things for love ; but how deep is his sympathy for the knowledge cult his way of urging the lesson proves clearly enough. It is in *Paracelsus* (the work that posterity will probably estimate as Browning's greatest) that we must look for the strongest proof of his sympathy with man's

desire to know and bend the forces of nature to
his service.  To some students this magnificent
work will appear only the  string of  pearls and
precious stones that some of us consider *Sordello*
to be.   To others it is a drama  illustrating the
contending forces of love and knowledge, others
again find in it only an elaborate  discussion
on  the  Aristotelian and Platonic systems of
philosophy ; it is none of these alone ; rather,
if a single sentence could describe it, it is the
Epic of the Healer, not of the hero who stole
from heaven a jealously-guarded fire, but of him
who won from heaven what was waiting for a
worthy recipient to take and help us to.   In so
far as Paracelsus came short, it was deficiency of
love that hindered him ; of his striving after
knowledge and what he won for man, the epic
tells in words and music that to me at least
have no equal in the whole range of literature.
At its full value does the poet appreciate the
God in man, the knowing Spirit which man is
only now beginning to dare look in the face.
Dreaded by theologians and hated by all the
Churches, from the Eden legend to the last
Encyclical, the story is ever the same : Knowledge is dangerous to man, and faith is all.   In

*Paracelsus* the thing condemned is not knowledge without faith but knowledge without love, to—

> "Know, not for knowing's sake,
>   But to become a star to men for ever;
>   Know for the gain it gets, the praise it brings,
>   The wonder it inspires."

Paracelsus has a message for our time. The tragedy of knowing without loving is often enacted now; and where the intellect is dissevered from the heart the end will be hard to keep from madness.

Wisdom demanded of Paracelsus—

> "Wilt thou adventure for my sake and man's
>   Apart from all reward?"

If the man of science cannot inscribe on his banner "Apart from all reward," he is not fit to enter the service of man. Says Tyndall: "Imagine Dr. Draper spending his days in blowing soap-bubbles and in studying their colours! Be it remembered it was thus that minds like those of Boyle, Newton, and Hooke were occupied, and that on such experiments has been founded a theory the issues of which are incalculable."—*Tyndall, "Light,"* p. 66.

The World knows little of the work done by men who long to—

> " Save mankind,
> To make some unexampled sacrifice
> In their behalf, to wring some wondrous good
> From heaven or earth for them, to perish, winning
> Eternal weal in the act; as who should dare
> Pluck out the angry thunder from its cloud,
> That, all its gathered flame discharged on him,
> No storm might threaten summer's azure sleep ! "
>
> *Paracelsus*, p. 62.

Yet in a thousand laboratories and students' cells this is being done at the present moment by men who have "all our varied appetites for joy derived from common things." "Men whom every common pleasure of the world affects as ourselves," but who "dare aspire to *know*—that in itself alone shall its reward be, not an alien end blending therewith ! "

It is most remarkable, that long before the scientific men of our time had given Paracelsus credit for the noble work he did for mankind, and the lasting boon many of his discoveries conferred upon the race, Mr. Browning, in this wonderful poem, recognised both his work and its results at their true value, and raised his reputation at this late hour from the infamy with

which his enemies and biographers had covered
it, and set him in his proper place amongst the
heroes and martyrs of science. We owe the
poet a debt of gratitude for this rehabilitation.
No man could have written this transcendent
poem who had less than Browning's power of
thrusting aside the accidents and accretions of a
character, and getting at the naked germ from
which springs the life of the real man. That
no follower of medicine, no chemist, no disciple
of science, did this for Paracelsus is, in the
splendid light of Mr. Browning's research and
penetration, a remarkable instance of the fact
that the unjust verdicts of a time and a class
need to be reversed in a clearer atmosphere,
and in freedom from class prejudice not often
accorded to contemporary biographers. A
poet alone could never have done us this
service; and a single attentive perusal of this
work is enough to show that the intimate
blending of the scientific with the poetic faculty
could alone have effected the restoration. How
lovingly the poet has taken this world's bene-
factor's remains from the ditch into which his
profession had cast them, and laid them in his
own beautiful sepulchre, gemmed, chiselled, and

arabesqued by all the lovely imagery of his fancy, no reader of Browning's *Paracelsus* needs to be told.

It might have been a Sir Charles Bell who wrote the lines on the Human Hand. Browning must have a knowledge of its structure more than skin-deep.

> " Flesh and bone and nerve that make
> The poorest, coarsest human hand
> An object worthy to be scanned
> A whole life long for their sole sake."
>
> *James Lee's Wife.*

Of the painter who is an anatomist he says—

> " To him the bones their inmost secret yield,
> Each notch and nodule signify their use ;
> On him the muscles turn, in triple tier,
> And pleasantly entreat the entrusted man :
> ' Familiarize thee with our play that lifts
> Here, and then lowers again, leg, arm, and foot ! '
> —Ensuring due correctness in the nude."

Even the mysterious technicalities of a medical prescription are not hidden from our poet ; he knows the principles upon which an intelligent physician proceeds, when he writes one—

> " Ask, now, a doctor for a remedy !
> There's his prescription.   Bid him point you out

Which of the five or six ingredients saves
The sick man.   Such the efficacity ?
'Then why not dare and do things in one dose
Simple and pure, all virtue, no alloy·
Of the idle drop and powder?'   What's his word ?
The efficacity, neat, were neutralized ;
It wants dispersing and retarding,—nay,
Is put upon its mettle, plays its part
Precisely through such hindrance everywhere :
Finds some mysterious give and take i' the case,
Some gain by opposition, he foregoes
Should he unfetter the medicament."
        *Prince Hohensteil Schwangau,* p. 78.

I will not trouble you with explaining how accurate this is, but I may say it is a precise statement of the methods that guide the pharmacologist, and affords the poet an admirable illustration of the method of our education and development in a world of contending forces and a pilgrimage of dangers and difficulties that, rightly met, subserve perhaps the highest interests the Great All-Father had in view for us when He placed us in their midst.

Browning's optimism is in complete accord with the teachings of science.   James Hinton, in one of his pregnant sentences, says, " Every evil, every failure or loss, becomes tributary to a greater good."

Browning declares that—

"Evil's beautified in every shape."

" Upon men's own account must evil stay."

" For mankind springs salvation by each hindrance inter-
posed, they climb."

Pessimism has no place in his system of
philosophy.

" Time means amelioration, tardidly enough displayed,
Yet a mainly onward moving, never wholly retrograde."

*La Saisiaz.*

As the unused muscle wastes away, the un-
exercised brain daily grows feebler and feebler,
and all the powers of man's body demand
exercise if they are to be retained in their in-
tegrity ; so, in Browning's system, evil is our
stimulus, whereby we evolve all the good we
can hope to get from this our mortal life.

The character of Count Guido, in the *Ring
and the Book*, is drawn with scientific accuracy,
and is elaborated with precision and great skill.
He has the true aspect of the ingrained villain,
a man who could not help being one.   A jury,
composed of nineteenth-century Royal Acade-
micians and physicians would have consigned
him to a criminal lunatic asylum.   I am sorry

we have not his skull on the table to-night. You would have found the facial angle extremely small, and doubtless some very interesting facts accounting for his character could have been discovered. Count Guido has left us his picture, painted by himself :—

> " Wipe out the being of me
> And smear my soul from off the white of things I blot ;
> I am one huge and sheer mistake.
> Whose fault ?   Not mine, at least,
> Who did not make myself."

Pompilia's sketch gives us his photograph :

> " Guido Franceschini—old
> And nothing like so tall as I myself,
> Hook-nosed and yellow in a bush of beard,
> Much like a thing I saw on a boy's wrist,
> He called an owl and used for catching birds."

No doubt the family history of the Count would give us some adequate reasons for concluding that he was in very truth " one huge and sheer mistake."

There is nothing " miraculous " (as has been said) in the stainless purity and beauty of Pompilia's character. The poet's abounding faith in Nature, his optimism and faithful observation of character, have drawn for us in Pompilia, a lovely, but by no means an impossible picture. Her character, we are told, taken in connection with her surroundings and parentage, is marvellous. As we do not read that her father was an habitual drunkard, or that her mother was either the subject of strumous diathesis or a microcephalic idiot, the marvel is not very apparent to the scientific mind. Her mother followed the calling of a washerwoman, and was probably a well-developed, healthy person.

Now, given good development and initial vitality at its best, Nature is very successful in continuing the species on the highest lines, quite regardless of ecclesiastical ceremonies or parochial registrations. Disclaiming any, the least desire to undervalue the importance of either, many reasons might be given why Nature so often uses such material with triumphant success ; certain it is that those who have the best reasons for knowing, often find Pompilias in very unlikely surroundings. To those who often become weary of trying to elevate other minds to their own level, it should be a source of satisfaction that it is well-nigh as difficult to efface the image of the Divine in man as to restore it when obscured by vicious habits and evil tendencies, for which their possessors cannot always fairly be held responsible. After all, education and environment do not effect so much either of good or evil as we often suppose. Otherwise in the homes of the brutal, the sensual, and the degraded, we should not find so many bright, innocent, and pure natures ; nor in the families of the high-born and cultivated, so many degraded types.

To some temperaments it is just as difficult to be evil as to others to be pure and good.

The characters of Guido and Pompilia are then perfectly natural. When the soul of Pompilia came within the path of Guido's, we find the repulsion that evil ever has for good.

> " And when he took my hand and made a smile—
> Why—the uncomfortableness of it all."

Bad men are often repugnant to good dogs.

To the man who refuses to believe in God, because he cannot find Him with his telescope, and whose microscope reveals Him not, Robert Browning declares—

> " The Name comes close behind a stomach cyst,
> The simplest of creations. . . .
> . . . The small becomes the dreadful and immense."
>
> *Sludge*, p. 203.

To him who will not believe in soul because his scalpel cannot detect it, he says, Show me first an atom! Immortality incredible? Your atom is a truly immortal being!

In one of the finest passages in *Ferishtah's Fancies* he discusses this difficulty, which the materialist has to face.

"To know of, think about—
Is all man's sum of faculty effects
When exercised on earth's least atom, Son!
What was, what is, what may such atom be?
No answer! Still, what seems it to man's sense?
An atom with some certain properties
Known about, thought of as occasion needs,
—Man's—but occasions of the universe?
Unthinkable, unknowable to man.
Yet, since to think and know fire through and through
Exceeds man, is the warmth of fire unknown,
Its uses—are they so unthinkable?
Pass from such obvious power to powers unseen,
Undreamed of save in their sure consequence!
Take that, we spoke of late, which draws to ground
The staff my hand lets fall : it draws, at least—
Thus much man thinks and knows, if nothing more."

*Ferishtah*, p. 131.

When we reflect how infinitely little we know of these atoms here spoken of, and of that mysterious force of gravitation, and the medium through which it acts, referred to in the last lines, it is not surprising we should be unable to solve the greater problems of life, the soul and God.

If it be contrary to received notions that in Browning we have a scientific poet, is it not still more remarkable that in a scientific man we have faith in some at least of the great doctrines of the Christian religion ?

Would not his dissecting, analysing spirit prove a solvent for creeds ? If we knew him less we might also predicate this of him. Nothing, however, could be more contrary to the fact. Again and again he warns us that we must not put religion into an alembic, must not resolve faith into its elements, analyse the pearl of great price, pump all the air out of the great Christian verities. In a word, he tells us "a scientific faith's absurd—frustrates the very end it was meant to serve" (*Poems*, vol. v., p. 170).

"You must mix some uncertainty with faith, if you would have faith be" (*Poems*, vol. v., p. 168).

He complains of the "exhausted air-bell of the critic"—that it "leaves no air to poison" (*Poems*, vol. v., p. 149), consequently none to

breathe, "pumps out with ruthless ingenuity
atom by atom, and leaves you—vacuity."
He tells us of the Göttingen professor, who,
with strange inconsistency, but exactly as our
Comtist and Agnostic philosophers are always
doing —

> "had done his best;
> And the pearl of price, at reason's test,
> Lay dust and ashes levigable
> On the Professor's lecture table.
> When we looked for the influence and monition
> That our faith, reduced to such condition
> Be swept forthwith to its natural dust-hole,—
> He bids us, when we least expect it,
> Take back our faith,—if it be not just whole
> Yet a pearl indeed, as his tests affect it."
>
> Vol. v., p. 156.

Which is exactly what our new lights are doing
with Christianity—grinding it to an impalpable
powder, and bidding us take the greatest care
to sweep up what they have left and religiously
conserve it. But fine dust is not a pearl; and
carbon, hydrogen, and oxygen in pint measures
are not exactly a loaf of bread. We cannot
adorn ourselves with the one, nor feed ourselves with the other. Browning tells us—

> "The originals of faith  .  .  .
> The causes, were they caught and catalogued,

Would too distract, too desperately foil
Inquirer.   How may analyst reduce
Quantities to exact their opposites
Value to zero, then bring zero back
To value of supreme preponderance ?
How substitute thing meant for thing expressed ? "
*Red Cotton Night-cap Country*, p. 196.

Yet he has some words of stern rebuke for Religion, that remind us of Dr. Draper framing his terrible indictment against her for her constant opposition to Science.   How she sat :

" Prim in place, Religion overlooked
And so had done till doomsday, never a sign
Nor sound of interference from her mouth,"—

while the rack pulled bone from bone, and the followers of Science were mauled and maimed. When Science became too strong for Religion longer to suppress, after first looking around for help not forthcoming, Religion acquiesced :

" What, broken is the rack ?   Well done of thee !
Did I forget to abrogate its use ?
Be the mistake in common with us both ! "

And the indignant poet turns upon her and cries :

" Ah but, Religion, did we wait for thee
To ope the book,   .   .   .
We should wait indeed !
That is all history."
*Ring and Book*, vol. i., p. 52.

R. B.                                               I

I saw once in Madrid, a few hundred yards
from the scenes of the medieval autos da fé, a
ballet, *The Genius of Progress contending with
Superstition.* In one scene a monk incites the
people to destroy the first steam-boat and its
inventor. That done, in the next, Progress
waved her wand, and a Mississippi water-palace
bore her thousand passengers on the wave. I
thought of Browning and the lines in *Pietro,*
how "the priests came prying, broke his en-
gine up, and bastinadoed him beside."

But if we culled from the works of Mr.
Browning all the passages that prove the per-
meation of his mind by the scientific habit,
we should weary you, even if we have not
already done so. The passages quoted are
ample to show that, whatever our notions of
poets and poetry may be in relation to science,
we have in Browning a writer who is abreast
of the highest culture of his time, who clothes
hard, dry facts of science in highly poetical
language, and invests their conception with all
the glamour of his art, extracting from a soil
usually considered unpromising, luxuriant
growths of most exquisite fancy, and above
and beyond all this, one of whom we may say,

in his own terse and pregnant lines, that we
may—

'Confidently lay to heart, and lock in head our life-long,
    this :
He there with the brand flamboyant, broad o'er night's
    forlorn abyss ;
Crowned by verse, and wielding, with wits' bauble, learn-
    ing's rod,
Well ?   Why, he at least believed in soul, was very sure of
    God."

---

## APPENDIX.

IT has been thought advisable to append some references to Mr. Browning's method of dealing with
scientific matters, that readers may have an opportunity both of seeing how wide is the poet's acquaintance with such things, and judge for themselves what
is his attitude toward science in general.   The list
of references makes no pretension to be an exhaust-
ive one, it could be considerably amplified by a
careful reperusal of the works, but it will suffice for
the purpose.   The references are to the original
edition of the poems, in six volumes, and the first
edition of the *Ring and Book.*

> *Anatomy.*—Poems, v., p.  152 ; vi., p.  58.   Fifine,
>    p. 68.
>
> *Astronomy.*—Prince H. S., p. 90.   Sordello, pp. 187,
>    188.
>
> *Botany.*—Poems, i., p. 104 ; v., pp. 193, 208, 228
>    312.   Fifine, p. 14.   Sordello, p. 20.

*Chemistry.*—Poems, iii., pp. 219, 220; iv., p. 238; v., pp. 155, 156. Prince H. S., pp. 44, 91. Red Cotton, p. 196. Croisic, pp. 90, 92. Fifine, pp. 65, 97, 130; Ferishtah, pp. 39, 40, 45, 76. Pippa P., p. 250. Sordello, p. 194. Ring and Book, i., p. 2.

*Electricity.*—Poems, vi., pp. 183, 203. Red Cotton p. 196. Fifine, p. 115.

*Evolution.*—Poems, i., p. 188. Prince H. S., p. 68. Fifine, p. 162. La Saisiaz, p. 57.

*Light.*—Poems, iii., p. 170. Jocoseria, p. 124. Fifine, pp. 65, 29. Numpholeptos, p. 101. Ring and Book, i., p. 71; iii., p. 170; iv., pp. 57, 79.

*Materia Medica and Therapeutics.*—Pietro of Abano, p. 84. Prince H. S., p. 77. Paracelsus, p. 111.

*Medicine.*—Poems, iv., p. 273; v., p. 220; Dramatic Idylls, ii., preface; Red Cotton, p. 199; Ferishtah, pp. 27, 55, 56. Ring and Book, iv., p. 12.

*Pharmacy.*—Poems, iii., p. 96; v. p. 220.

*Physiology.*—Poems, v., p. 191. Sordello, p. 195. Tray.

*Scientific Matters in General.*—Poems, v., pp. 128, 302; vi., p. 203. Dramatic Idylls, ii., p. 68. Fifine, pp. 51, 86. La Saisiaz, pp. 69, 82. Ferishtah, p. 131. Sordello, pp. 25, 203; Ring and Book, iv., pp. 61, 77, 180.

Considerable discussion was caused amongst Browning students by the publication of my paper on this subject. Amongst other communications two letters from distinguished literary women were published in the *Browning Society's Notes and Transactions.* I here venture to republish them with my reply, as the question is a very interesting one, as bearing upon the idea which Mr. Browning has done so much to dissipate, that poetry must necessarily be all sugar and water.

BROWNING AS A SCIENTIFIC POET.—"I don't think I could do a more cruel turn to a poet than to prove him to be scientific, or to have displayed his scientific acquirements in his poetry!

For why? Because—*selon moi*—

1st. The scientific way of viewing all things is precisely the converse of the poetic. The scientific is analytic—the poetic synthetic; the man of science is busy finding out distinctions and tracing causes—the poet ought to be engrossed in the aspect of resemblances, comparisons, appearances. Think of any poem super-eminently poetic—*e.g.*, *The Sensitive Plant.* Imagine *that* treated scientifically. Describe the plants as cryptogams and phenogams, monandria and polyandria. Cut out all such unscientific folly as describing the Lily of the Vale made pale by passion, or the Hyacinth ringing sweet peals from its bells, and the Narcissus admiring itself in the water. The difference between your botanic garden and Shelley's garden will be exactly the difference, I think, between scientific poetry and true poetry.

2nd. I believe that the emotions—which it is the business of all Art, but chiefly of the greatest Art,

poetry, to stir and elevate—are in their nature complementary to the intellect, which is the realm of
science ; and that in proportion as the one part of
our nature is being excited, the other is temporarily
quiescent. The alternations may be rapid, and we
may slip from a high peak of intellectual climbing
on to an Alpine rose-bed of rich emotion ; but this
is an exceptional chance, and the rule, I apprehend,
is that *busy thought* is *cold feeling*, and *vice versâ.*

Are we, therefore, to lay it down that poetry ought
not to deal with subjects intellectually difficult or
abstruse ?

It seems very hard to draw the line, and I cannot
profess to say I could formulate a rule to my own
satisfaction, much less for that of others. But I
think the principle must be, that there should never
be required of the reader (assuming him to be a fairly
cultivated man) to stop in mid-career of a burst of
poetry to say, 'What the deuce does this poet mean?
What *is* this substance—this plant—this disease—
this author—this battle—of which he is talking?'
Recourse to a lexicon or a cyclopædia is the very
last thing which a poet should even suggest to his
readers. Thus, I should say that when a fact of
science (*e.g.*, that the earth goes round the sun) has
become *familiarly known*, it is open to every poet
to speak of the earth's motion accordingly. But
it would not have been proper to do so in Shakespeare's days, and it would not now be well to intro-
duce the Precession of the Equinoxes into an ode.
In like manner, as everybody now knows something

about the saurians, Tennyson was quite right to talk of

> 'Dragons of the prime
> Which tare each other in their slime.'

But if he had gone on to speak of the dental formula of the Labyrinthodon, it would have been the reverse of poetic.

I must say I think it is *too* audacious coolly laying it down, that 'only in an age of science can anything worthy of the name of poetry exist.' Shades of Isaiah, Homer, Æschylus, Dante! He does well to make the most of Lucretius—the only poet of the past who (so far as I know) can be described as scientific at all, and whom it is the fashion in these days to laud to the skies, both because he is scientific and because he is atheistic.

Is there not a rule which applies to Art of every kind, and, of course, to Poetry *par excellence*, that it ought, as its supreme end, to excite the emotion of the *Beautiful?* According to my idea, the concern of Literature is with the True—of Art with the Beautiful, and, of course, with all emotions which may be associated with the sense of Beauty—Pity, Terror, Admiration, Awe, etc. When anything is introduced into Art which calls forth the opposite emotions—the sense of disgust, of *mesquinerie*, pettiness, and ugliness—it is the antithesis of Art, and, so far as it goes, a direct subtraction from it—*e.g.*, when Rubens represents a dog lapping the blood in the brazen pan in his 'Crucifixion.'

Now I maintain that several of the examples given
of Scientific Poetry involve this direct offence against
the fundamental principle of Art. The epidemiologist hunting up cholera bacilli may (or may not)
be *morally* great, but he is æsthetically beastly!
When Browning talks of the child "ichoring" over
the place where he had felt God (as if God left a
scab!) it makes one think of a nasty little itchy child,
and to shiver! I could not feel *poetry* for three pages
after such a metaphor."

Z.

BROWNING AS A SCIENTIFIC POET.—"Dr. Berdoe
undeniably uttered a paradox when he said that
Browning, as poet, was gifted with the scientific habit,
and pursued the scientific method, of thought; and
'Z.' has delivered himself of as obvious a truism, in
declaring that the poetic and the scientific method are
incompatible. But this is little more than a question
of words. What Dr. Berdoe *meant* must be sought
in the general drift of his assertions, and tested by
the works to which they refer; and the smallest effort
in this direction will reveal two facts : that when Dr.
Berdoe speaks of scientific *thought*, he is thinking of
scientific *imagination :* of 'the deeper insight into
the hidden things of nature,' which is not always
combined with the 'highest poetic faculty,' but
seems a natural complement to it; and that in calling
attention to the scientific element in Mr. Browning's
imagination, he reaffirms that profound truth to
nature which is the secret of Mr. Browning's poetic

power. It is a mistake to think, as 'Z.' apparently
does, that Science and Poetry are opposed to each
other. Their received antithesis lies, not in the things
themselves, but in the minds which pursue them : in
the habit of mind, which, in its lower stages, the
pursuit of science involves. The higher scientific
truths belong to the imagination ; they are elicited
by it ; they exist in and for it. Their province is
therefore that of the poet ; they have their natural
analogies in poetry. Mr. Browning's employment of
scientific facts is always inspired by these analogies,
whatever the special quality of the facts may be ;
and Dr. Berdoe shows, by both quotation and com-
ment, that it is so. The lines given by him from
*James Lee's Wife* display a knowledge of anatomy
reducible to the lower planes of science ; but they
form part of an almost impassioned tribute to the
wonders of the human frame—its embodied gospel
of Work—its embodied lesson of reverence, patience,
and self-effacement. *Deaf and Dumb* and *Numpho-*
*leptos* are each a parable of the laws of light. Neither
could have been written before the prism was known.
But the one contains in its few lines a spiritual philosophy of life. The suggestiveness and the glamour
of true poetry reach their climax in the other. The
word 'ichor,' to which 'Z.' so much objects, signifies
in the present case the ethereal fluid which was supposed to supply the place of blood in the veins of the
gods. It belongs to the purest poetry of waste and
repair ; and any reference which 'Z.' may see in it
to the condition of an itching or scabby child must

be charged to his own mind. That the discoveries of
science are the property of the poet's imagination is
further proved by this, that it can on occasion fore-
stall them. The quoted passage from *Paracelsus*
is a poetic statement of the doctrine of Evolution
made long before its scientific basis had been laid
down ; at a time when it was still blasphemy to speak
of Creation as otherwise than accomplished in the
course of six days and out of nothing.

'Z.' employs a poem of Shelley's, *The Sensitive
Plant*, to illustrate the anomaly of carrying the
ideas of science into poetry. 'Imagine,' he says,
'*that* treated scientifically. Describe the plants as
cryptogams and phenogams, monandria and polyandria. Cut out all such unscientific folly as describing
the Lily of the Vale made pale by passion, or the
Hyacinth ringing sweet peals from its bells, and the
Narcissus admiring itself in the water. The difference between your botanic garden and Shelley's garden
will be exactly the difference, I think, between scientific poetry and true poetry.' I venture to reply that
if the plants were only described as 'Z.' 'imagines,'
by their botanical terms, the result would be a scientific report, and not a poem at all ; but that if they
were described, as Browning might describe them,
in the activities which these terms denote : in the
romance, and the mystery, and the humanity of their
reproductive existence, we should have a poem at
least as genuine as one which invests them with fanciful attributes, dealt out as the mood of the poet or
the swing of the verse suggests.

'. . . the Naid-like lily of the vale,
Whom youth makes so fair, and passion so pale,'

sounds charming so long as we do not stop to ask
ourselves why the lily should resemble a nymph, and
yet be always pale with passion ; or whether it is
nice for such a young person to be so ; but the idea
is feeble at best when compared with that of Browning's sunflower, in *Rudel to the Lady of Tripoli*, of
which the vivid and pathetic human imagery con-
veys a natural fact. I have no wish to disparage
Shelley, who has written finer things than *The
Sensitive Plant,* and given us even here finer, because
truer, images than two out of three of those which
'Z.' quotes. Nor would I speak disrespectfully of
the great poets of a less scientific age ; though I
fancy that if we approached their works in the same
spirit in which we read those of our own time, a
little of them would sometimes go a long way. I
agree with 'Z.' that Christopher North overstates
his case when he asserts that, 'Only in an age of
science can anything worthy of the name of poetry
exist.' But I entirely feel with Dr. Berdoe, that that
poet must be the greatest whose genius reflects in
fullest union the passions which are of all time, and
the mental experiences which characterize his own ;
and that the poet of the scientific age is, other things
being equal, by so much greater than his predecessors, that he inherits the longest past, and therefore
the richest present, and reproduces it.

It would, however, be sophistry to deny that other
things seldom *are* equal. If the scientific age creates

the best materials for poetry, it also creates the worst
atmosphere for it ; were it only that it produces a
large class of readers who refuse themselves to the
faintest effort of imagination. ' Z.' is of opinion
' that there should never be required of the reader
(assuming him to be a fairly cultivated man) to stop
in mid-career of a burst of poetry to say, " What the
deuce does this poet mean ?   What *is* this substance
—this plant—this disease—this author—this battle—
of which he is talking ? "   Recourse to a lexicon or a
cyclopædia is the very last thing which a poet should
even suggest to his readers. . . .' So am I. But
what compels the reader of Browning, in three cases
out of four, to have recourse to the cyclopædia,
except his own belief, that the things and facts in
question mean nothing unless they are to be found
there : his inability to admit that, whether real or
imaginary, their relation to the main idea, *i.e.*, their
illustrative value, is the same ?   Mr. Browning is to
blame for this in some of his works, because their
illustrations are often too remote to convey the intended idea ; but even where his poetic intention is
transparent, the same demand for chapter and verse
is made upon him. ' Imagine ' *The Sensitive Plant*
read in the same manner as those poems of his
to which the last issue of the Browning Society's
*Queries* refers, and the kind of speculations concerning it which a Shelley Society would bring to
light. ' Was the garden suggested by any particular
garden ? ' ' Was the lady suggested by any particular lady ? ' ' Where did Shelley probably locate

the garden?' 'Is a garden possible which contains plants and flowers requiring such different soils and atmospheres?' 'Of what species of sensitive plant is the one described?' . . . to say nothing of all the questions involving just criticism which are raised by the often arbitrary images or imperfectly marked ideas of the poem."

O.

The criticism of " Z." in the last number of *Notes and Queries* is so able that I should not have found anything to object to in it had I felt sure it was directed against what I did say in my paper on Browning as a scientific poet, instead of being an elaborate argument against what I did *not* say. In the first place, I did not maintain that Browning treats poetic subjects scientifically, but scientific matters poetically—quite another thing. Neither is there any question of "display" in his method. The scientific habit is as natural to him as his poetry. One does not "display" a pair of beautiful eyes—I thought I had made this clear. " Z.'s " argument, if it proves anything, proves too much—it proves that Browning is not a poet at all! We are told, "the scientific way is analytic," "the man of science is busy finding out distinctions and tracing causes." Is not the *Ring and the Book* analytic? Does not the poet there busy himself "finding out distinctions and tracing causes"? There is plenty of analysis in that poem—and plenty of poetry too. This is just what Browning students always claim for him, that

he does "find out distinctions and trace causes," and
some of them think all this enhances his claim as a
poet. I apprehend there is a great difference between
the scientific method and its terminology. I purposely excluded "the cryptogams and phenogams,
monandria and polyandria," when I said, "Not in
the sense satirized in the *Loves of the Plants*, but
in the fact that he has so largely imbibed and *assimilated* the science of .the time." To me the latest
revelations of botanical science are infinitely more
suggestive of poetry than the fables of Ovid about
the origin of trees and flowers. Is that only poetic
which deals with the unreal and absurd ? I am
unable to say what is the temperature of people who
"slip from a high peak of intellectual climbing on to
an Alpine rose-bed of rich emotion." Unhappily,
we sometimes are called to poor men who slip from
housetops on to iron railings ; in these cases the
"cold feeling" is undoubted. "Z." lays down a
canon that poetry does not become such till people
are able to understand it without lexicons and cyclopædias. So there is hope for Mr. Browning yet !
When the Board Schools have done a little more
for us, we shall discover our poet. But to be logical,
"Z." should at least admit him to be a poet to those
who do understand him now. If that is not true
poetry which cannot be properly understood without
cyclopædias and dictionaries, how about Dante ?
What proportion of his readers could understand
him without some such notes as Carey's ? And is
there not a Shakespeare Society that affords very

19. Warwick Crescent.
W.
June 11. '85.

Dear Dr Berdoe,

I have again to express my sense of the obligation your goodness lays me under by the Paper in which you so generously estimate my attempts to make use of the few materials of a scientific nature I have had any opportunity of collecting: would they were of more im= =portance! — but my gratitude to whoever takes the will for the deed is all the greater. Pray accept my sincere thanks, and believe me,

dear Dr Berdoe,
yours truly ever
Robert Browning

considerable help to his students? Isaiah, Homer, and Æschylus want explanation, too! It was not I, but Christopher North, who said, "Only in an age of science can anything worthy of the name of poetry exist." He goes on, in my quotation, to say that uncivilized man has not produced any poetry worth "a tinker's farthing." Commenting on this passage "Z." exclaims, "Shades of Isaiah, Homer, Æschylus, and Dante!" Neither I nor North claimed the present as the only age of science; still further from our thoughts would it be to designate those poets as "uncivilized" men. "Z." says "Lucretius was the only poet of the past who can be described as scientific at all." What about Michael Angelo and Goethe?

Leonardo da Vinci very successfully combined his science with art, too, even if he did not write poetry, as Raffael did—indifferently.

"Z.'s" essay on poetry is very clever and very interesting, but it is not a criticism of my paper, as it is directed against a line of argument not advanced therein.

E. BERDOE.

The letter on the opposite page was written by Mr. Browning after the publication of my paper on his scientific allusions.

# BROWNING'S SCIENCE.

A GREAT poet, fully conversant with the science
of his time, in sympathy not only with the aspirations of his age, but with its intellectual
progress, must necessarily exercise an influence
upon the educated and thoughtful far beyond
that possessed by poets, however great, whose
only object is to express artistically the emotions of the human mind in rhythmical language. Many eminent writers have maintained
that science and poetry are opposed to each
other, and that as the one flourishes so must
the other decay. The poet, they say, deals
with resemblances, comparisons, appearances ;
in a word, with the beautiful and its relations
to the emotions of pity, terror, admiration, awe,
etc. The scientist, on the other hand, occupies
himself with finding out distinctions and tracing
causes ; in a word, with facts. According to
these, it is little less than libellous to write of a
poet that he is scientific, or of a man of science
that he is poetic ; it is in either case to detract

from the honour attaching to his proper work.
If the ornithologist were to intrude himself
upon us while we were enjoying *The Ode to
the Nightingale*, or the poem of *The Sky-
lark*, we should resent it as a personal affront.
Who cares for meteorology when revelling in
*The Cloud*, or for botany when delighting in
*The Sensitive Plant?* Nothing is easier than
to ridicule the idea of introducing genera
and species, cryptogams and phenogams, into
such associations as those of Shelley's *Garden*.
This sort of thing has been done to perfection in *The Botanic Garden* and *The Loves of
the Triangles*. Nevertheless, we maintain
that, other things being equal, the poet who
knows his natural history, his botany, and his
physical science will write better poetry than
he who knows nothing of these things. He
will not, of course, worry us with his classifica-
tions and analysis, but his deeper penetration
into the mysteries of Nature will enable him to
impress us more entirely with a sense of his
truth to Nature, of his nearness to and harmony
with Nature in all her varying moods and
phenomena. I may be pardoned for this intro-
duction to what I have to say on Browning's

R. B.                                        K

science, because I have for some years past
occupied myself with pointing out to Browning
students in England how much Browning's
scientific imagination and learning enhance the
value of his poetic work and his claims to recognition as a great teacher of the nineteenth
century.   Browning's work is as distinctly the
product of the age of science as Petrarch's of
the revival of learning.

No prophet can speak to the heart of his age
who is out of sympathy with its work and
hopes.   Would he lead the minds of his time,
he must know their thoughts and speak them
better than they can themselves.   He must
invest himself in their mental dress and dignify
it by his mode of wearing it; must take their
crude longings and intimations and transmute
them with the philosopher's stone of his genius
into the gold of burning, shining thought, which
shall dower the ages with a heritage for ever.
He must not set himself to scold and scorn
his age nor denounce the "down-grade" tendencies of its earnest, passionate thought; out
of harmony with it, he can effect no good.   To
lead, he must love; to love, he must know.
That Robert Browning is a great poet, it is

happily now too late to deny. It concerns me
at present to indicate some of the reasons for
estimating his work as part of the worthiest
literary product of our time. Macaulay says
that "the merit of poetry, in its wildest form,
still consists in its truth." It is obvious that,
to be true, a poet cannot know too much.
Now there is not a mood of the human mind,
from the mental agitation of a Pope debating
high matters of Church and State to the squirm-
ing of a Sludge detected in his contemptible
fraud, which is beyond the power of Robert
Browning to analyze and explain. He is not
only the heroes' poet or the singer of rounde-
lays and the idyllist of empty days. It is the
"poet's trade to feign," says Churchill; but
Browning's work is rather to divine the hidden
things of the human soul for us and open to us
the hieroglyphics of nature. Analysis with
him becomes inventive; he is "the maker"
because he is so great an analyst. He unwraps
and dissects so skilfully that the power of
synthesis has come to him from the perfection
of his knowledge of the materials in which he
works. Take, for instance, his *Paracelsus;* so
perfectly did he take to pieces the old myths

and legends about this reformer of medicine, that he has been able to reconstruct for us what is acknowledged by men of science to-day as the truest history of the man. See what he did with the meagre scraps of history of Count Guido Franceschini. He pulled that faded, worn, old book to bits, put it into the alembic of his brain, and distilled for us *The Ring and the Book*, which is doubtless much truer for us than would have been the actual facts and words seen by coarser eyes and heard by duller ears. Thus does analysis lead with genius such as his to synthesis ; and for this I call him a scientific poet.

This is a consolatory fact, because it shows us that the progress of science need not be fatal to poetry. We shall understand our materials so much better, that we shall make more out of them. The chemist is the great manufacturer precisely because he is the great separater and resolver. Campbell said :—

> " When science from Creation's face
>     Enchantment's veil withdraws,
> What lovely visions yield their place
>     To cold material laws ! "

But is it so ? Tennyson speaks in one of his

poems of the "white star of snow"; before
Mr. Glaisher's observations on snow-crystals
he would have had to call it a "flake." There
are many instances in the Laureate's works
of the influence which modern scientific discoveries have exercised upon his genius.
Browning's poems, however, teem with them,
and this possibly is one element in their
obscurity. It cannot be denied that one wants
educating up to Browning; but the process will
undoubtedly pay. In *Ferishtah's Fancies*
he speaks of the human ear as "hungry for
music." We shall miss the poet's meaning
unless we know something of the organ of
Corti, with its three thousand rods, the beautiful arrangement of which has been compared
to that of the keys of a piano. In the next
line he speaks of the "seven-stringed instrument" before the eye; here the reference to
light and the seven colours of the spectrum is
more obvious. In *Hohenstiel-Schwangau* we
have the lines :—

> "Try to make good do good as evil does—
> Were just as if a chemist, wanting white,
> And knowing black ingredients bred the dye
> Insisted these too should be white, forsooth !"

Those experimenters with chemicals, who have
made the beautiful white and blue fires out of
black antimony and sulphur, will know what
the poet means. In *Easter Day* there is a
very remarkable illustration of Plato's maxim,
that "poets utter great and wise things which
they do not themselves understand." He
says :—

> "Thy choice was earth : thou didst attest
>     'Twas fitter spirit should subserve
>     The flesh, than flesh refine to nerve
>     Beneath the spirit's play."

This poem was written five years before
Herbert Spencer gave the first hints as to the
origin of the nervous system in medusæ. He
points out how an impression or stimulus
comes to habitually traverse a certain path
along the lines of least resistance, thus leading
to a differentiation of the protoplasm. Mr.
Bastian has shown how the constant repetition
of such a process has gradually produced the
" nerve fibre." How did the poet anticipate
this great scientific discovery ? Those students
of the poet who are interested in the study of
the science of optics will have remarked the
important place which his light metaphors hold

in his poems. " Red, green, and blue that whirl into a white." . . . "The prism's obstruction shows aright the secret of the sunbeam." . . . "Light thwarted, breaks a limpid purity of rainbow flakes." In *Fifine* he speaks of losing "the varicolor in achromatic white." *Numpholeptos* is quite unintelligible without some acquaintance with optics.

How wonderfully he anticipated recent discoveries in evolution and embryology in his *Paracelsus* I have lately had occasion to explain. Though holding no brief for any of the Churches, it cannot be doubted that Mr. Browning is a Christian poet. His theology is so eminently reasonable that it commends itself to a large class of minds which have forsaken the Churches because modern criticism has laid rude hands on the dogmas, creeds, and documents upon which they are grounded. The study of comparative religions, the sciences of folk-lore, anthropology, and psychology have dissipated much of the supernatural which forms so large a portion of the older religious teaching. The great want of the age is a faith which is adequate to and consistent with its intellectual culture. I venture to think that such a system

of reasonable religious belief is to be found in
the works of this great writer.  I hail it with
joy, not so much for its own completeness
and perfection as for its indication of the
direction in which we must look for the religion of the future.  It is vain to deny that we
live in a transition period as far as our faith is
concerned.  Many of the Churches resemble
those wooden buildings in India which have
been the prey of the white ant—they retain all
their outward form and appearance of strength,
but they will not resist the next high wind, for
they are eaten through and through by the
destroying insect.  Churches and religious systems and societies, however, may collapse ; but
the "indestructible religious need" of the human race will be satisfied by a commensurate
theology when even their very names are forgotten.  In the beautiful words of Lotze, the
great German philosopher, "The totality of all
that has value—all that is perfect, fair, and good
—cannot possibly be homeless in the world or
in the realm of actuality, but has the very best
claim to be regarded by us as imperishable
reality."  Man has often found that he has outgrown his gods ; he will never outgrow such a

conception of God as that! He may part with
his anthropomorphic conceptions of the Supreme Being; but "the mind which meditates
in Beauty and speaks in Law" will ever be
adored by thinking men. And we can worship
Browning's God without loss of our self-respect.
To do this he tells us we must—

> "Correct the portrait by the living face,
> Man's God by God's God in the mind of man."
>
> *The Ring and the Book.*—The Pope.

To Browning "God is the perfect Poet, who in
His person acts His own creations," . . .
"tastes an infinite joy in infinite ways," and
"dwells in all, from life's minute beginnings up
at last to man." In God is life for evermore,
yet existence in its lowest form includes Him,
as he tells us in the noble passage in *Paracelsus*, from which I quote. No one can read
this without looking upon nature with "larger,
other eyes." Matter is no longer the dead
thing of the laboratory; it is "a crystallized
thought of God." He cannot conceive that the
All-powerful and All-wise could fail to—

> "prove as infinitely good :
> Would never, with power to work all love desires,
> Bestow e'en less than man requires."
>
> *Christmas Eve.*

It is not incomprehensible, therefore, to him
that—

> "This one earth, out of all the multitude
> Of peopled worlds, as stars are now supposed,—
> Was chosen, and is sun-star of the swarm,
> For stage and scene of Thy transcendent acts,
> Beside which even creation fades
> Into a puny exercise of power."
>                     *The Ring and the Book.*—The Pope.

He can believe that "the very God," "the All-
great," may be "the All-loving too,"—

> "For the loving worm within its clod
> Were diviner than a loveless god
> Amid his worlds."

But why does God never speak ? He stands
by, and, seeing all the evil and misery in the
world, does nothing to stay it ! How reasonable is Browning's answer. He says that
God—

> "stands away
> As it were a handbreadth off, to give
> Room for the newly-made to live,
> And look at him from a place apart,
> And use his gifts of brain and heart."

The process of man's education could go on in
no other conceivable manner. Man, otherwise,
would not be man,—he would be a mere

machine, " Made perfect as a thing of course,"
but " his liberty of doing evil gave his doing
good a grace." " I see no sign of God," says
the scientist ; " I can explain everything without Him ! " Browning does not take him to
the stars above, he bids him look through the
microscope at —

> " the simplest of creatures, just a sac
> That's mouth, heart, legs, and belly at once, yet lives
> And feels, and could do neither, we conclude,
> If simplified still further in degree."

And what then ? Why, " The Name comes
close behind a stomach cyst," which is the
designation the biologist gives that simplest of
all living things which the poet has described ;
and this arrest of knowledge exactly indicates
the high-water mark of the science of the day.
The Name—God—is immediately behind that
stomach cyst!—behind that veil we cannot peer,
and the latest scientific word is, that there is not
the least probability that we shall ever bridge
the gulf between the not-living and the living.
There stands science confounded—" thus far
shalt thou come, and no farther." But if we
boast that, though we cannot solve the mystery
of life, we have mastered matter, " No ! " cries

the poet, "the mere atoms despise" you! the
awful, eternal atoms which no man hath seen
nor can see, of whose ceaseless dance Tyndall
has told us, of their linking and breaking away
and whirling on unceasingly in their infinite
combinations, ever changing yet never being
lost. Of all this must we think ere we can
sound the depth of the meaning,—"the atoms
despise" us.

Conversing recently with one of our greatest
English divines, he said to me, the words, "The
Name comes close behind a stomach cyst," con-
veyed no idea whatever to his mind; and he
adduced that as one of his reasons for thinking
Browning obscure. This gave me the opportunity of pointing out to him that if he had
spent a small fraction of the time he had devoted to Greek particles to learning the elements of biology, he would not have so unjustly
condemned the poet. This is a good illustration of the mental preparation which is demanded in a Browning student. Is the fault
with the poet? By no means. A good
preacher has a right to good listeners. Professor Max Müller recently said, that neither
Tennyson nor Browning could be understood

without an acquaintance with the Greek and
Roman classics ; this is presupposed in our idea
of an educated person.  In Browning's case a
knowledge of the physical sciences is also demanded of us ; but this only shows that Browning is in advance of his time, as a leader of men
should be.  The age cannot be very distant when
an acquaintance with science will be as common
as a knowledge of the ancient classics : then
we shall hear less of Browning's obscurity.
Browning's theory of life is eminently in accord
with the teachings of evolution and development.  At first the savage merely lives the
animal life; in time he comes to learn *how* he
lives,—

> " and the more he gets to know
> Of his own life's adaptabilities
> The more joy-giving will his life become."

The very failures of our life prove it to be an
advance from a lower form, as the poet shows
in *Cleon.*  " The moral sense grows but by
exercise," and if it be true that " an honest man
is the noblest work of God," it is impossible to
imagine how he could have attained his nobility
by any other means than the " training and
passage " of this life.  Browning's theory of

life is scientific because he goes into its purpose ;
and what to the pessimist is infinite mystery is
replete with law and order to him. Poor
atheist Thompson, who wrote *The City of
Dreadful Night*, exclaimed,—

> "I find no hint throughout the universe
> Of good or ill, of blessings or of curse ;
> I find alone necessity supreme.

> "The world rolls round for ever like a mill ;
> It grinds out death and life, and good and ill ;
> It has no purpose, heart, or mind, or will."

It was natural that such pessimism should lead
to the Lethe of opium and alcohol, and the
melancholy end in the wards of the hospital.
To the healthy mind of Browning—

> "This world's no blot—
> Nor blank : it means intensely and means good."

The evolutionist has taught us many things
as to the origin and development of bodily
organs. It is not more certain that necessity
has gradually produced and improved these
than that—

> "As with body so deals law with soul,
> That, stung to strength through weakness, strives for good
> Through evil."

The pessimist who fails to see all this is like

a colour-blind person who cannot find the beauty of the rainbow. It is not the bow in the clouds which wants colour, it is his deficiency of the colour-sense which is to blame. Looking back at the history of our race, we can find no noble deed, no heroic effort, which could ever have sprung from the pessimist's gloomy creed. Mental health means optimism. This is the oxygen of the soul, and there never was a brave and valiant effort made without it. The fatal choke-damp of the poets of the Leopardi and Schopenhauer school finds no place in the robust pages of Browning. It vitiates much of the work of Shelley, Byron, and Heine, but probably no poetic atmosphere so nearly approaches mountain air as his. If anything, it is too strong for most of us in the old world. The newer blood and stronger lungs of the new world breathe it with greater pleasure.

Contemplating the lower forms of life, the poet sees that they have arrived at perfection; the star-fish is complete,—no better star-fish seems required,—but he sees—

> " Man, for aye removed
> From the developed brute ; a god though in the germ."

On this he grounds his belief in the immortality of the soul :—

" Life is probation, and the earth no goal
But starting-point of man ; compel him strive,
Which means, in man, as good as reach the goal."

God, the soul, the future life ; earth, the school-
time ; love, the one great lesson to learn ;
character to be evolved from the contest with
evil ; the substratum of good in every soul
which leaves always some possibility of restoration ; the imperishable nature of all good and
the ever-diminishing sum of evil,—these are
the high themes of the poet's work, and there
is nothing grander in the intellectual condition
of our time than to see this noble, robust, old
Anglo-Saxon standing amidst the wrecks of
the creeds and the crumbling ruins of the
Churches to proclaim that all which is best
and most instinct with life and power in our
religion is based on eternal fact, and nowise
to be shaken by criticism or disturbed by the
progress of the ages.   This man speaks to us
with authority, " Crowned by prose and verse
and wielding with wit's bauble, Learning's
rod,   .   .   .   he at least believes in soul
and is very sure of God ! "

# PARACELSUS:
## THE REFORMER OF MEDICINE.

LET us go back in thought to the middle of the
fourteenth century, which saw the birth of the
period known as the Renaissance or Revival
of Learning, and which preceded the dawn
of the Reformation. The early part of the
century was the glacial period of European
thought; all real intellect was enchained in
"thrilling regions of thick-ribbed ice." The
religious condition of Europe at this time is
familiar to every student of history. It is with
science we have now to deal. For nearly
two thousand years the philosophy of Aristotle had reigned supreme over all Europe.
Hallam tells us that "what the doctors of the
Middle Ages had been in theology, that was
Aristotle in all physical and speculative science,
and the Church admitted him into an alliance
of dependency for her own service." From
the domination of this system, which kept the
human mind in bondage, there seemed no

escape. Men had grown to love their thral-
dom. But this philosophical deity was not
the real Aristotle, but Aristotle converted to
Christianity and dressed in a monk's frock.
The world had worshipped the sage as a
Hebrew, then as a Moslem, now as a Christian
and a pedant. Knowledge in the schools
"revolved like a squirrel in a cage;" henceforth, after two thousand years of turning about
upon itself, it was to progress.

If religious thought was restricted and con-
trolled, science was bound hand and foot and
hidden in darkest dungeon. Pietro of Abano,
the greatest philosopher and physician of the
preceding century, was so successful in curing
diseases, so skilful a builder and astronomer,
that he was held to be a wizard, and condemned to be burnt alive. This was the
common reward of any who ventured to take
a single step forward on the path of human
progress.

Less known than the martyrs of religion, the
noble army of the martyrs of science have
perhaps a greater and more lasting claim upon
our gratitude. The former found in their faith
itself its own supreme reward; they were

upheld by its transcendent support and were sustained by supernatural consolations. The martyrs of science had nothing to cheer them but the sad smile of truth and the consciousness that their vindication was ultimately secure. The Reformation was but a portion, and that by no means the most important part, of the great Renaissance; it was a natural outgrowth of the Revival of Learning. This may be said to have commenced in 1453, when Constantinople fell into the hands of the Turk. "The new learning now began to awaken free thought," says Mr. Symonds; "it encouraged curiosity, and prepared the best minds of Europe for speculative audacities from which the Schoolmen would have shrunk, and which soon expressed themselves in acts of cosmopolitan importance." The great melting period of the glaciers was from 1492 to 1500. Columbus discovered America, and the passage to India was found. Printing was growing into vigour, and the art of war being revolutionized by the invention of gunpowder, and the discoveries of Copernicus had effected no less a revolution in the science of cosmology. Luther was born in 1483. Ten years later

Paracelsus, the Luther of medicine and of chemical science, was born at Einsiedeln, near Zurich. It is not hard to recall these Reformation scenes as one stands on the Rhine bridge at Basle, watching the tumultuous flow of the river, itself formed by the melting of the ice and snow of the Alps above. We naturally think, as we stand there, of another breaking up of ice, and the source and progress of another river taking its rise in these lands. Close by the Rhine we see the cathedral in which are the tombs of Erasmus and Œcolampadius and other pioneers of modern thought; but the Browning student's reflections will be centred on the University buildings close by the bridge. At this University Paracelsus—the first teacher, be it remembered, who ever held a chair of physical science—worked and taught in 1526; here he was nicknamed " Luther Alter "—the other Luther. Up to the time when, in 1835, Mr. Browning wrote his poem *Paracelsus*, the world had nothing but a distorted image of the hero, which was, in fact, little better than a caricature drawn by his bitter enemies. Mr. Browning's vast research amongst contemporary records has enabled him to put together

—like Professor Owen with his prehistoric bones—a consistent and faithful figure of the real man. When Mr. Browning says, in the notes appended to the poem, that the liberties he has taken with his subject are very trifling, we now know this to be the fact, because we have access to the documents which confirm his estimate of the hero's life. In all history it would be difficult to find another character which has been so slandered and misrepresented as that of Paracelsus. He was the son of a physician, William Bombast von Hohenheim, who taught him the rudiments of alchemy, surgery, and medicine; he studied philosophy under several learned masters, chief of whom was Trithemius of Spanheim, Abbot of Wurzburg, a great adept in magic, alchemy, and astrology. Under this teacher he acquired a taste for occult studies, and formed a determination to use them for the welfare of mankind. He could hardly have studied under a better man in those dark days. Tritheim himself was well in advance of most of the teachers of his time. As it is impossible to place ourselves in full sympathy with Mr. Browning's hero unless we have some idea

of the perplexing and much misunderstood
subject of alchemy, I may be pardoned if I
make a short quotation from a book of this
same Johannes Trithemius, printed at Passau
in 1506. He says: "The art of divine magic
consists in the ability to perceive the essence
of things in the light of Nature, and by using
the soul-powers of the spirit to produce
material things from the unseen universe
(A'kasa), and in such operations the Above
(Macrocosm) and the Below (the Microcosm)
must be brought together, and made to act
harmoniously. The spirit of Nature is a unity,
creating and forming everything, and by acting
through the instrumentality of man it may
produce wonderful things. Such processes
take place according to law. You will learn
the law by which these things are accomplished
if you learn to know yourself. You will know
it by the power of the spirit that is in yourself,
and accomplish it by mixing your spirit with
the essence that comes out of yourself." By
this we see that Tritheim was of the theo-
sophists or mystics, for they are of the same
class, and probably, in their German form,
derived their origin from the labours of Tauler

of Strasburg, who afterwards, with "the Friends of God," made their headquarters at Basle. The mysticism which is so dear to Mr. Browning, and which finds its highest expression, perhaps, in the poem which we are considering, is not therefore out of place.

The poem opens with a touching scene, where the hero is parting from his beloved friends, Festus and Michal, on the eve of his departure from home, to wander, as was the custom, from University to University as a poor scholar "aspiring to know."

His self-will, his dissatisfaction with his teachers, his mysterious promptings to gain knowledge in some original way, lead his friends, who represent the conservative type of mind, to implore him to stay at home.

> "Stay with us ! Cast those hopes away
> And stay with us !
> Man should be humble : you are very proud :
> And God, dethroned, has dreadful plagues for such ! "

But Paracelsus, though protesting that he is no misanthropist, declares that his "vast longings" urge him forward. Sorcery and magic do not content him as the means of penetrating the

secrets of Nature; he will leave the schools
and henceforth be taught of God,—

" Who summons me to be His organ."

And so, leaving "the region of abstractions,
fictions, visions, spectral hopes and fears, in
the midst of which the intellect," as Mr.
Symonds says, "somnambulistically moved
upon an unknown way," he goes forth from
the little town of Einsiedeln, following the star-
gleam of truth, and hearing what he thinks to
be the voice of God—because having heard it,
go he must :—

" Be sure they sleep not whom God needs,"

he says.

"Why not stay here and learn ?" they
ask ; "converse with the mighty dead, fill out
their unfulfilled careers, take up their unsolved
problems.    Snatch the torch from the tired
runners and bear it onward ! You will have
no books in the desert, you will find no foot-
prints in the caves where you will be the first
visitor !  In the ruined cities where wisdom
would not stay, in the ravaged towns which
renounced her,"—

"Rejecting past example, practice, precept,
Aidless 'mid these he thinks to stand alone ! "

Yes ! he accepts all that : he says, —

" I seemed to long
At once to trample on, yet save mankind,
To make some unexampled sacrifice
In their behalf, to wring some wondrous good
From heaven or earth for them, to perish winning
Eternal weal in the act ; as who should dare
Pluck out the angry thunder from its cloud,
That, all its gathered flame discharged on him,
No storm might threaten summer's azure sleep."

In these prelusive notes we have Mr. Browning's overture to the drama of " Paracelsus: Hero and Martyr of Science." We shall find all these recur again and again in the harmony to follow.

Mr. Ruskin somewhere divides mankind into three orders of beings : " The lowest, sordid and selfish, which neither sees nor feels ; the second, noble and sympathetic, but which sees and feels without concluding or acting ; the third and highest, which loses sight in resolution and feeling in work." To this latter class did Paracelsus belong. " I go to prove my soul ! " " I shall arrive ! " he cries. When a man of this sort comes to feel that

way, go forward he must. As Carlyle says :
" Some arrive ; a glorious few ; many must be
lost, go down upon the floating wreck which
they took for land. Nay—Courage! These
also, so far as there was any heroism in them,
have bequeathed their life as a contribution to
us, have valiantly laid their bodies in the chasm
for us ; of these also there is no ray of heroism
*lost*, and on the whole, what else of them could
or should be 'saved ' at any time ? Courage,
and ever forward ! "

We next see Paracelsus in the house of
a Greek conjuror at Constantinople. Here
Paracelsus *attains*. It is nine years since he
took the diver's plunge for the pearl. Has
he secured it ? solved the mystery of being,
reached the grand secret of life ? He had
not even found its elixir, nor the philosopher's
stone, nor the universal solvent. He had
discovered modern medicine and the science
of chemistry ; but though it cannot be said he
was unaware of the great consequences which
must follow these discoveries, it is certain that
he underrated them in comparison with what he
had hoped to have achieved. When he left his
home, he went to study in the mines of the

Tyrol. That was seeing his way without much circuit first ; there he was in the region of fact ; if he extracted metals, it must be with pick and shovel instead of cabalistic formulæ. No coaxing and wheedling Nature there, but a fight and a struggle for her treasures. We are told that he learned mining and geology and the use of metals in the practice of medicine. " I see," he says, " the true use of chemistry is not to make gold, but to prepare medicines."

In his sermon on the world's unknown benefactors, Cardinal Newman asks, " Who gave us the use of the valuable medicines for the healing of disease ? " and he implies that the inventors are mostly unknown. We shall see what Paracelsus did in this direction. He is rightly termed "the father of modern chemistry." He discovered the metals zinc and bismuth and hydrogen gas, and the medical uses of many minerals, the most important of which were mercury and antimony. He gave to medicine the greatest weapon in her armoury—opium. His celebrated azoth some say was magnetized electricity, and others that his *magnum opus* was the science of fire. He acted as army surgeon to several princes in

Italy, Belgium, and Denmark. He travelled
in Portugal and Sweden, and came to England;
going thence to Transylvania, he was carried
prisoner to Tartary, visiting the famous colleges
of Samarcand, and went thence with the son of
the Khan on an embassy to Constantinople.
All this time he had no books. His only book
was Nature; he interrogated her at first-hand.
He mixed with the common people, and drank
with boors, shepherds, Jews, gipsies, and
tramps, so gaining scraps of knowledge wherever he could, and giving colourable excuse
to his enemies to say he was nothing but a
drunken vagabond, fond of low company. He
would rather learn medicine and surgery from
an old country nurse than from a University
lecturer, and was denounced accordingly and—
naturally. If there was one thing he detested
more than another, it was the principle of
authority. He bent his head to no man.
Surely never was there a man with such a
wolf-hunger for facts of his own acquisition.
And now, estimating all his labours at so low
a value, he can go on no longer, and we find
him in the magician's house in Constantinople,
in search of the universal panacea, if you please.

He is in despair, thinks he has done nothing. The process is too slow for him, though we know he had already done so much. He will learn now by supernatural means, diabolical perhaps, because the process is quicker. He must have rest, too, for his throbbing pulses and gnawing heart. Life and strength are going; he has atrophied his once human heart by purging it of love, and has subdued his whole life to the one purpose to know. Has he been fighting sleep for death's sake perhaps? Is he losing his reason?

> " 'God, thou art mind! he cries;
> Crush not my mind, dear God.' "

He learns the secret; he is told that he has missed his life's end by refusing Love, as another lost one has missed his by refusing Knowledge; they two are " halves of one dissevered world."

Love saves others, and self-sacrifice is the surest way of saving one's self. " He alone," says a mystical writer, " who loves, has and is Christ, having in virtue of his love the ' Dissolvent' and the secret of 'Transmutation' in respect of the whole man. Krishna has his Arjun, Buddha his Ananda, Jesus his

John—terms denoting the feminine and tender
moiety of the Divine nature." He has learned
that true knowledge does not consist in accumu-
lating it for its own sake, but in distributing its
fruits in loving work for men. Henceforth the
ideal must give place to the actual service as
the first condition of the highest internal illumi-
nation. To what extent are we to consider
this scene at Constantinople historical ? The
poet's purpose is easy enough to trace. The
reformer, the truth-seeker, the cold speculative
philosopher has somehow to be brought into
sympathetic relations with his fellow-men ; he
has burned up his human affections in his
furnaces, and has cast away as dross his human
heart-promptings. As love cannot reach him
otherwise, a direct revelation must be vouch-
safed to him. Mr. Browning has to convert
his ascetic scientist (who has only given up
gold making and the search for the philosopher's
stone because he sees that a wider and simpler
chemistry promises better results) into the
successful healer, the blessed physician of the
poor and the giver of health to princes ; and he
does not see a better way of converting him
than by revealing the Gospel of Love to him

in a magician's house. There does not appear
to be any historical basis for this scene between
Aprile and Paracelsus. The real Paracelsus,
as we find him in his works, was full of love
for humanity; and it is much more probable
that he learned his lesson while travelling, and
mixing among the poor and wretched, and
while a prisoner in Tartary, where he doubtless
imbibed much Buddhist and occult lore from the
philosophers of Samarcand, than that anything
like the Constantinople drama was enacted.
Be this as it may, we have abundant evidence in the many extant works of Paracelsus that he was thoroughly imbued with the
spirit and doctrines of the Eastern occultism,
and was full of love for humanity. A quotation from his *De Fundamento Sapientiæ*
must suffice : " He who foolishly believes is
foolish ; without knowledge there can be no
faith. God does not desire that we should
remain in darkness and ignorance. We should
be all recipients of the Divine wisdom. We
can learn to know God only by becoming wise.
To become like God we must become attracted
to God, and the power that attracts us is love.
Love to God will be kindled in our hearts by

an ardent love for humanity; and a love for
humanity will be caused by a love to God."
It would not have been so dramatic, but I
would rather, I confess, have seen Paracelsus
slowly working this out for himself amongst
his peasants and miners and fellow-soldiers and
prisoners, than having it revealed to him as to
Saul at Damascus by miracle.    I am not quite
sure though that this is all that Mr. Browning
means us to learn by this scene.    May it not
be that the great Reformation of the sixteenth
century is composed of the art-loving, sensuous,
Aprile-like Renaissance, or revival of polite
learning, and the scientific awakening which
took place in Germany after Luther's Reformation ?    Lorenzo de Medici might in this connection be the Aprile, and Paracelsus the
representative of the scientific spirit.    I merely
throw this out as subject for discussion.
Lorenzo seems very well indicated by the
speech of Aprile beginning : " I would love
infinitely and be loved."

In the year 1525 Paracelsus went to Basle,
where he was fortunate in curing Froben the
great printer by his laudanum when he had
the gout.    Froben was the friend of Erasmus,

who was associated with Œcolampadius ; and
soon after, upon the recommendation of Œcolampadius, he was appointed by the city mag-
nates a professor of physics, medicine, and
surgery, with a considerable salary; at the
same time they made him city physician, to
the duties of which office he requested might
be added inspector of drug-shops. This ex-
amination made the druggists his bitterest
enemies, as he detected their fraudulent practices ; they combined to set the other doctors
of the city against him ; and as these were
exceedingly jealous of his skill and success,
poor Paracelsus found himself in a hornets'
nest. We find him then at Basle University
in 1526, the earliest teacher of science on
record. He has become famous as a physician,
the medicines which he has discovered he has
successfully used in his practice ; he was now,
in the eyes of his patients at least,—

"The wondrous Paracelsus, life's dispenser,
Fate's commissary, idol of the schools and courts."

In the poem he is once more conversing with
his friend Festus, who is congratulating him.
But he declares that he has not been successful,

R. B.                                              M

and really is at heart most miserable ; his very popularity galls him, he feels he is but a zany in a show; public flattery he despises ; the incense of the ignorant mob he has never sought ; he knows that all this is lowering his mental tone, he is being converted into a quack against his will. Festus reminds him that death retires before his presence, that his skill has often availed to raise "the shattered frame to pristine stateliness," that pain-racked men by his blessed opiate may swoon into a sea of bliss, that he is ordained to free the flesh from fell disease as Luther frees the soul. Men say it is done by magic and such folly; it is however done ! Arrogant ? Yes, he admits that men may say that of him. He did begin his lectures at Basle by lighting some sulphur in a chafing dish and burning the books of his great predecessors in the medical art, Avicenna, Galen, and others, saying : " Sic vos ardebitis in gehennâ." He boasted that he had read no books for ten years, though he protested that his shoe-buckles were more learned than the authors whose works he had burned. Yet notwithstanding these sentiments he is not inclined to see anything but defeat, when, after aiming at comprehending God Himself, His works, and all His intercourse with the human mind, he finds himself with life passing away and strength failing, a mere lecturer to " beardless boys, and bearded dotards worse."

It must have been a wonderful spectacle when this new teacher took his place before his pupils. The benches, occupied hitherto by a dozen or two of students, were crowded with an eager audience anxious for the new learning. Literature had been exhumed many years before, and now it was the turn of science! Fancy it, students in the nineteenth century, what honour to have been seated on one of these groaning benches assisting at the disentombment of physical science! Leaving the morbid seclusion of the cloisters, men had given up dreaming for inquiry, and baseless visions for the acquisition of facts. This was the childhood of our science, and its days were bright with the poetry of youth. " You Italy, you Dalmatia, you Sarmatia, Athens, Greece, Arabia, and Israel! Follow me—come out of the night of the mind!" he cries. It is a sight to arouse our enthusiasm, to see in the early dawn of our modern science this man standing up alone to pit himself against the whole scientific authority of his day. He rises from the crucibles and fires where his predecessors had been vainly seeking for gold and silver, ever and again pretending to have found them and always going empty-handed to a deluded world; henceforth, he says, his alchemy shall serve a nobler purpose than gold-seeking, it shall aid in the healing of disease. He casts aside the sacred books of medicine which have been handed down the ages by his predecessors; destroying them, he declares, with an earnestness which is less tinged by arrogance than by conviction, that these men had been blind guides, that he alone has the clue of the maze; and he forsakes all to follow truth, though she lead him to death. In his generous impulse to serve mankind he has spoken harshly of his opponents. They would not have helped him any way. He was above them, they could not understand him, so they hated him, and he scorned them. As too often happens to such heroes, he forgot the love of his neighbour in his love for mankind.

And here we cannot help pausing to ask

how it was that the art of medicine had failed
to make any progress whatever from the
earliest Christian times? Paracelsus found his
pupils holding fast by the teachings of the
School of Salerno, founded by the Arabs; and
there seems no ground for supposing that the
healing art had made the slightest progress in
Europe from the foundation of that school in
1150, except in that branch known as pharmacy. For this stagnation the Catholic Church
was chiefly to blame. She enjoined the care
of the sick no doubt, but she did nothing to
further the progress of medical science; the
principal remedies were prayers and relics.
Not that there was any scarcity of doctors;
there were plenty of Greek, Arabic, and Jewish
physicians; but none but rich and powerful
persons dare call in their services for fear of
excommunication. Benedict IX. and Urban
II. in the eleventh century ordered that clerical
physicians should only practise within the walls
of their monasteries. Neither prelates nor any
of the superior clergy were permitted to practise in any branch of medicine. The ignorant
and often sensual lower clergy were allowed
to act as physicians; but even they were for-

bidden to engage in surgery, for the expressed
reason that the Church abhorred the shedding
of blood. Teeth-drawing and bleeding were
relegated to the lay brethren who were the
servants and the barbers of the community;
and no doubt from this circumstance we derive
the title of barber-surgeons, the extremely
interesting history of which body has just been
published in the " Life of Vicary," where the
story of the foundation of Bartholomew's Hospital is told by our President, Dr. Furnivall,*
and his talented son, Mr. Percy Furnivall, who
is a distinguished pupil of that school of
medicine; these gentlemen have done a great
service to the history of medicine in England
by their labours in that work. Why did
the Church oppose the study of medicine?
The answer is simple. In those days everything which tended to withdraw the veil of
mystery from the secrets of life was considered
to have a tendency to destroy religion. The
Church seemed unwilling to have the secrets
of life explained. Everything which tended
to account for the processes of being and the

---

* This paper was read before the Browning Society.

causes of health and disease was so much with-
drawn from the privileges of the Church.
Paracelsus had burst his bonds, had in some
marvellous manner come to see that a clean
sweep must be made of all this Arabian, Kab-
alistic, Scholastic rubbish before he could begin
to teach anything. On the day that he stood
up before that audience at Basle University he
was to write the first lines of the principles of
rational medicine. Do you grudge him a clean
slate? Away then with "Ætius, Oribasius,
Galen, Rhasis, Serapion, Avicenna, Averroës,"
and the other blocks. To the influence of
relics, theological conjuration, and all the
ridiculous and often disgusting remedies of his
professional brethren he had opposed his
scientific common-sense method of dealing with
disease. He had saved the life of a prince
who was at first grateful; but when the monks
had pointed out that a want of respect had
been shown to the Sudarium of our Lady, and
the abbey where it was kept had been de-
frauded of its dues by this indecently hasty
cure, the convalescent prince had to prove his
orthodoxy by burning a dozen heretics straight
away in the public square; and he would doubt-

less have burned Paracelsus too for sorcery
had he not escaped from his power. They
had sent him diplomas, he tells his friend
Festus, and presents from Germany, France,
and Italy, and what he valued more than
these : he had received a letter from Erasmus,
whose friend Frobenius, he says, he had raised
from the dead. But all these things are a
poor solace at best; and he confesses that a
host of petty, vile delights now supply the
place of his dead aims, "as sickly fungi spring
from the roots where tall trees used to flourish."
Then his first desire infinitely to know comes
back in all its force, and he declares—

> " Would God translate me to His throne, believe
> That I should only listen to His word
> To further my own aim ! "

He has fallen low, but though he cannot soar
he will not crawl ; he knows that he precedes
his age, he has bartered sleep in vain.

They tell him there is another world to
remedy the ills of this ; but he bursts out :—

> " Another world !
> And why this world, this common world, to be
> A makeshift, a mere foil, how fair soever
> To some fine life to come ?
> .     .     .     .

No, no ;
Love, hope, fear, faith—these make humanity ! "

In 1528 we find him at Colmar in Alsatia.
He has been driven by priests and doctors from
Basle ; he says woefully :—

" Poor Paracelsus is exposed
At last ; a most egregious quack he proves."

He had been called to the bedside of some
rich cleric who was ill ; he cured him, but so
speedily that his fee was refused. Though not
at all a mercenary man (for he always gave
the poor his services gratuitously), he sued the
priest; but the judge refused to interfere, and
Paracelsus used strong language to him, and
had to fly to escape punishment. We must
not be too hard upon the canon. Disease was
treated with profound respect in those days,
and great patients liked to be cured with de-
liberation and some ceremonial. Heart-broken
and indignant at the world's ingratitude, Paracelsus now declares he will moderate his aims,
abandon his vast ambitions, live the common
life, cast out his lovely fancies, and earn his
grave, for mind is only disease and natural
health is ignorance. He is desperate—he

chants the song of the men who "clung to
their first fault and withered in their pride."
The closing scene of the drama is laid in a
cell in the hospital of Salzburg. It is the year
1541, his age but forty-eight; and the divine
martyr of science lies dying. Recent investigations in contemporary records have proved that
he had been attacked by the servants of certain
physicians who were his jealous enemies, and
that in consequence of a fall he sustained a
fracture of the skull, which proved fatal in a
few days. There is nothing in the whole range
of our literature grander or more beautiful than
this death-scene, as painted by Robert Browning. His faithful Festus, watching the weary
night long by the sinking champion of the
truth, prays for his recovery, for his salvation.

"Save him, dear God; it will be like Thee : bathe him
   In light and life ! Thou art not made like us ; "

He declares that,—

"Come weal or woe
His portion shall be mine. He has done well.
I would have sinned, had I been strong enough,
As he has sinned. - Reward him, or I waive
Reward ! If Thou canst find no place for him,
He shall be king elsewhere, and I will be
His slave for ever. There are two of us."

Turning to the dying hero he says,—

"God shall take thee to His breast, dear spirit,

.        .       .       .       .

And here on earth
Shall splendour sit upon thy name for ever—

.        .       .       .       .

Thee—the master mind,
The thinker, the explorer, the creator!"

The dying man sits up, must speak, must sing his death song. Once more he must wear his scarlet fur-lined robe, with his chain about his neck, and his trusty sword Azoth in his grasp. He reviews his life, owns his sins and his failure, owns too his pride and his unspeakable despair, laments that he had misunderstood his place and mission. Still he protests that he never fashioned out a fancied good distinct from man's.

"God is glorified in man,
And to man's glory vowed I soul and limb;
Afterwards they will know me."

Such is Mr. Browning's study of the Real Paracelsus, the Medical Ishmael. He was buried in the churchyard of St. Sebastian at Salzburg; but in 1752 his bones were removed to the porch of the church, and a monument was erected to his memory by the archbishop. When his body was exhumed it was discovered that his skull had been fractured during life. How different the story is from the previous caricatures in our biographical dictionaries a very little research will show. "Charlatan," "drunken empiric," "conjuror," "sorcerer," "quack," " extravagant impostor." This is how he was described before Mr. Browning wrote. He could read between the lines of his history, and was the first in our time who refused to accept the common story as true. If you refer to the article "Alchemy" in the last edition of the *Encyclopædia Britannica*, you will find that men of science now recognise Mr. Browning's great poem as a far truer estimate of the man's work than any we had previously. He had errors, but they were mainly the fault of his time; his virtues were his own. Was he a charlatan? Men have said so while appropriating his discoveries and passing them off as their own. Charlatans are not often great discoverers or inventors. A drunken empiric? because he frequented the society of common people, instead of watching his alembic in a lonely tower. His profession did not at all

approve of his delivering his lectures in the
vulgar tongue, in place of the Latin language ;
but this was part of his noble plan, and was
the beginning of free thought in science ; he
laboured for humanity, not for a profession.
He cured poor people without taking his fees ;
this was bitterly resented by his brethren.
Medical men did not then do as much work for
charity as they happily do now. He is gravely
charged with being an empiric, as if medicine
even at the present day were not largely em-
piricism. Sir Morell Mackenzie says as much.
But Paracelsus did more for scientific medicine
than perhaps any of its students. True, he
rejected anatomy ; but then he made the grand
discovery that Nature was sufficient for the
cure of most diseases. He was a Neo-Pla-
tonist, and considered the mind had more to do
with disease than the body. There was much
truth in that. " Imagination is the cause of
many diseases ; faith is the cure for all," he
says. Just this doctrine is being taught now
largely in America with some success, under
the name of " Christian science healing."

Mr. Browning seems too readily to admit
the charge of drunkenness so persistently

brought against his hero. In the 4th Scene he makes him accuse himself in the strongest terms. He speaks of his "heart, which God cursed long ago," as now a pet nest for devils. He speaks of his "degradation," of being "half stupid and half mad." We saw how, in the previous scene, he spoke of the host of petty, vile'delights which like fungi had usurped the place of his dead aims. This is dramatic, and it has some historical colour no doubt. Mr. Browning even gives us a note to the effect that "his defenders allow the drunkenness." But we ask, Is it reasonable? We know how this man's character has been misrepresented in so many ways—we can see that much of his so-called arrogance was inspiration, and inspiration so far beyond the conception of the narrow, bigoted, grossly ignorant monkish minds about him that the inspiration of genius was probably mistaken ofttimes for that of wine. We know how many charges his secretary Oporinus trumped up against him. May he not have largely exaggerated this account of his lecturing in a state of intoxication day after day? Is it reasonable? Consider the work the man did. Here we have some 106 treatises on Medicine,

Alchemy, Natural History and Philosophy, Magic, and other subjects, written within a period of time covering fifteen years. He had a great practice and crowds of pupils, was a constant and persistent persecutor of Nature for the purpose of extracting her secrets ; how could he have accomplished a work the value of which we are now only just beginning to appreciate, if he lived in that state of constant intoxication which Mr. Browning says his de-fenders admit ? We may guess how much of all this is true by remembering what certain historians have said of Luther, and indeed of all the Reformers. He was called an " ignorant vagabond." In truth he was no lover of books, and despised mere University learning. " The book of Nature," he affirmed, " was that which the physician should read, and to do so he must walk over its leaves." We pore over books now till our faculties of observation become atrophied. Paracelsus' library, we are told, consisted of a Bible, St. Jerome on the Gospels, a volume on Medicine, and seven manuscripts. So, as he travelled so much and read so little, what could the musty old pedants who spent their lives amidst the disputations of the School-

men consider him but an "ignorant vagabond?"
What are we to say about his magic and
astrology? There are two kinds of magic—
black and white. The former is devil worship,
the latter is synonymous with occult science, or
divine science, as it was sometimes called. Mr.
Browning makes his hero abjure the "black
arts" and the aid of "sullen fiends" and "fallen
spirits" in the outset of his career; and though
we find him soon after inquiring in the conjuror's house, it does not appear that the poet
has sent him thither to learn anything from the
devil, that would certainly be at variance with
anything we can discover in his authentic
works.* By magic in his writings we are to
understand, he says, "the highest power of the
human spirit to control all lower influences for
the purpose of good." He talks a great deal
of superstitious nonsense in this connection, but

---

* He seems to have had a very poor idea of the devil's
power. In his book entitled *Philosophia Occulta*, he says,
"The devil has not enough power to mend old broken
pots, much less to enrich a man." He goes on to say, "That
which is unexpected will in future prove to be true, and
that which is looked upon as superstitious in one century,
will be the basis for the approved science of the next."

there is no evidence of his dealing with the powers of darkness, as was of course charged upon him by the Church on account of his remarkable success. He was an alchemist, and alchemy stands in the same relation to modern chemistry that astrology does to astronomy. We should treat neither with contempt; they have too great a claim upon us for what they gave birth to. And here I must be permitted to touch briefly on the subject of the cosmology of Paracelsus. I dare say some of us have thought, when reading that wonderful death song which the poet puts into the mouth of his hero, that there was in it a great deal more of Mr. Browning than of Paracelsus. I confess I have often thought that myself; but a more careful study of the works and opinions of this thinker and explorer has convinced me that these lovely lines are quite in accord with what we may expect the real Paracelsus to have said. To fully understand the purport of the lines where the poet speaks of man as—

> " The consummation of this scheme
> Of being, the completion of this sphere
> Of life ; whose attributes had here and there
> Been scattered o'er the visible world before,

R. B. N

Asking to be combined, dim fragments meant
To be united in some wondrous whole,
Imperfect qualities throughout creation,
Suggesting some one creature yet to make,
Some point where all these scattered rays should meet
Convergent in the faculties of man,"—

and to see the reasonableness of thus making
Paracelsus talk evolution, we must know a
little of his cosmology and of his curious teaching about the Macrocosm and the Microcosm.
We know that his eagerness to understand the
relation of man to the universe led him to the
study of the Kabala, where this relationship is
attempted to be explained. Much of his vision-
ary cosmology has been evidently derived from
this curious Jewish work. The Kabala teaches
that the whole universe was incomplete, and
did not receive its finishing touch till man was
formed, who is the acme of the creation and
the Microcosm. In the *Zohar*, iii. 48, we
read : " As soon as man was created everything was complete, including the upper and
nether worlds, for everything is comprised in
man. He unites in himself all forms." By
the Macrocosm then we are to understand the
universe, including the visible and invisible
things ; by the Microcosm we mean the little

world, a term usually applied to man. It was held not only that there was a relationship between man and the forms of life below him, but also between his spiritual body and the planets, and on this Wiegel says : " The external heaven, with its continued revolution, hath a most convenient correspondency with the inward heaven in the Microcosm, and this with that." This was fully believed by Paracelsus ; and though to modern science it seems very absurd, the belief had a definite and useful influence. It is not quite so absurd perhaps as we may think. He says : " The human body is composed of primeval stuff," what we now term cosmic matter. Now the spectroscope has proved that the same chemical elements of which the earth and sun are composed are found in all the stars. In Haeckel's *History of Evolution* there is a series of plates illustrating the various consecutive aspects of the human embryon. These make up a perfect picture of the microcosmic development. If we were to place them side by side with Mr. Browning's lines, they would form their best commentary. (I wish the Browning Society would publish them.) This poem, we must

bear in mind, was written in 1835, twenty-three
years before Darwin and Wallace familiarized
the world with the doctrine of evolution.
"Nature," says the poet, "is nothing but a
thought of God reflected in the life of man." *

> "God is the perfect poet,
> Who in His person acts His own creations."

This is just the idea of the Kabalists and
Paracelsists; they say, "The material universe
is a thought of the Eternal Mind thrown into
objectivity by its will, and crystallized into
matter by its power"; to them "all stars and
mountain peaks are thoughts of the Eternal
Mind." † "The visible body of the invisible
God," says Paracelsus. Matter to him was not
dead. He says: "Matter is, so to say, coagu-
lated vapour, and is connected with spirit by
an intermediate principle which it receives from
the spirit."

We cannot understand Paracelsus and the
science of his time without a little inquiry as
to what was meant by the search for the philo-

---

* So Balzac: "Dieu est le poète," and Petronius: "Mundus
totus exercit histrionem."

† Dr. Hartmann's *Paracelsus.*

sopher's stone, the elixir of life, and the universal medicine. It is very difficult to discern what was really intended by these phrases. Dr. Anna Kingsford, who paid considerable attention to the hermetic philosophy, says : " These are but terms to denote pure spirit and its essential correlative, a will absolutely firm and inaccessible alike to weakness from within and assault from without." Another writer ingeniously tries to explain the universal solvent as really nothing but pure water, which has the property of more or less dissolving all the elements. His alcahest—as he termed it—as far as I can make out, was nothing more than a preparation of lime ; but writers of this school only desired to be understood by the initiated, and probably the words actually used meant something quite different. There was a reason for using an incomprehensible style, for fear -of the persecutions of the Church ; and these books, like the rolls in Ezekiel, were " written within and without." Many great truths, we know, were enshrouded in symbolic names and fanciful metaphors.

It is certain that Paracelsus, like his predecessors, sought to possess the elixir of life.

It does not appear from his writings that he thought it possible to render the physical body immortal; but he held it to be the duty—as the medical profession holds it still—of the physician to preserve life as long as possible. A great deal of matter attributed to Paracelsus on this subject is spurious; but there are some of his authentic writings which are very curious and entertaining. He describes the process of making the Primum Ens Melissæ, which after all turns out to be nothing but an alkaline tincture of the leaves of the common British plant known as the Balm, or *Melissa Officinalis.* Some very amusing stories are told of the virtues of this concoction by Lesebure, a physician to Louis XIV., and which speak volumes for the credulity of the doctors of those times.

Mr. Browning makes his hero say to his friend Festus, when he tells him that his wife Michal is dead,—

> " I have no julep, as men think,
> To cheat the grave ; "

and this little point is typical of the historical accuracy of the poet's work.

Another of his great secrets was his Primum Ens Sanguinis. This is extremely simple, being nothing more than the venous injection of blood from the arm of "a healthy young person." In this we see that he anticipated our modern operation of transfusion.

His doctrine of signatures was very curious and most absurd. He thought that "each plant was in a sympathetic relation with the Macrocosm, and consequently with the Microcosm." "This signature," he says, " is often expressed even in the exterior forms of things." So he prescribed the plant we call Euphrasy or " Eye-bright " for complaints of the eyes, because of the likeness to an eye in the flower; small-pox was treated with mulberries, because their colour showed that they were proper for diseases of the blood.

This sort of thing still lingers in country domestic medicine. *Pulmonaria officinalis*, or Lungwort, so called from its spotted leaves, looking like diseased lungs, has long been used for chest complaints. Michael Drayton, in his *Polyolbion*, describes one of the herbalists, and tells us how he went to work with his simples :—

" For them that are with newts, or snakes, or adders stung,
   He seeketh out a herb, that is called adder's tongue
   As Nature it ordain'd its own like hurt to cure,
   And sportive did herself to niceties inure."

As Emerson says :—

   "The old men studied magic in the flowers,
   And human fortunes in astronomy,
   And an omnipotence in chemistry,
   Preferring things to names, for these were men,
   Were unitarians of the united world,
   And, wheresoever their clear eye-beams fell,
   They caught the footsteps of the SAME."

Of course we see nothing of all this ; the plants
have nothing to tell us, since—

   " We ask their pottage, not their love."

Now-a-days this all seems very silly; but
we must not despise the ways we came by
our knowledge of things. Mr. Tyler says :
" Analogy has always been the forerunner of
scientific thought ; " and we know that even
magic had its uses in the beginnings of science.

What was the " cross-grained devil in my
sword " of which he tells Festus in the third
scene ? Mr. Browning says it was azoth, or
simply " laudanum suum." If so, why " cross-
grained devil ? " Writers on magic, of whom

Dr. Hartmann is one, describe azoth as being " the creative principle in Nature; the universal panacea or spiritual life-giving air — in its lowest aspects, ozone, oxygen, etc." Much ridicule has been cast upon Paracelsus for his belief in the possibility of generating homunculi, but after all he may only mean that chemistry will succeed in bridging the gulf between the living and the not-living by the production of organic bodies from inorganic substances. This may perhaps ultimately be done, though we know it has not hitherto been effected.

We must be to some extent familiar with the philosophy of Paracelsus. That Mr. Browning is a mystic I presume no one will deny; hence his sympathy with this mystical theosophist. Take, for example, the beautiful lines in the first part of the poem beginning—

" Truth is within ourselves.

.      .      .      .      .

There is an inmost centre in us all
Where truth abides in fulness; and around,
Wall upon wall, the gross flesh hems it in."

Before we can clearly see the idea expressed in these lines, we must know that Paracelsus held that the constitution of man consists of

seven principles : (1) The elementary body.
(2) The archæus (vital force). (3) The sidereal
body. (4) The animal soul. (5) The rational
soul. (6) The spiritual soul. (7) The man
of the new Olympus (the personal God).
Those who are familiar with Indian philosophy
will recognise this anthropology as identical
with its own.    Paracelsus, in his *De Natura
Rerum*, says : " The external man is not the
real man, but the real man is the soul in connection with the Divine Spirit."  We understand now what Mr. Browning means when
he says that knowing is opening the way to
let the imprisoned splendour escape.

He was called a quack and impostor because
he cured sick folk by unaccustomed methods.
We have baptized these methods now, and
given them orthodox names. Thus does the
quackery of to-day, like its heresy, become the
orthodoxy of to-morrow. We may forgive this
man his wrathful arrogance and boastfulness
"for the sake of the indomitable hardihood
with which he did lifelong battle, single-
handed, against enthroned prescription," says
a recent writer.  Into the tangled undergrowth
of theosophy, mysticism, magic, and theology,

he burst with the pioneer's hatchet of chemical experiment and clinical observation, and cleared a path for physical science. The path was narrow it is true, it led through many a dangerous place ; but it is the same road which greater engineers have improved for our use to-day. Here is your true Pathfinder and Pontifex Maximus ! He belonged to the highest order of men, that of the initiators who are the guides of mankind, who, bearing aloft the torch of intellect, plunge into the regions of the unknown, and call on us to follow them. New ideas to men of his type are as the oxygen we breathe—they cannot help doing great things. I said that some of his apparently absurd notions had a basis of truth. Let me give an instance of this : his idea that all Nature was living, and that there is nothing which has not a soul hidden in it—a hidden principle of life— led him to the conclusion that in place of the filthy concoctions and hideous messes that were in vogue with the doctors of his time, it was possible to give tinctures and quintessences of drugs, such as we now call active principles— in a word, that it is more reasonable and pleasant to take a grain or two of quinine than

a tablespoonful of timber. He set himself to
study the causes and the symptoms of disease,
and sought a remedy in common-sense methods.
Mr. Browning is right when he makes him say
he had "a wolfish hunger after knowledge ;"
and surely there never lived a man whose aim
was to devote its fruits to the service of
humanity more than his. After this brief
study of his life and character, how faithful
seems the estimate of the poet to the life-
passion of the hero!

What wondrous good has he brought, Pro-
metheus-like, from heaven ? Let me tell you
just one. A child was burned the other day
from head to foot; in terrible agony it was
taken to the hospital, in an hour it was calmly
sleeping. A man at work upon the front of a
house lost his footing, fell, was impaled upon
the railings ; he too was taken to the hospital,
in a short time he also was asleep. Both had
the blessed tincture of opium invented by.
Paracelsus ; and in Browning's words :—

> " Men in racking pains may purchase dreams
> Of what delights them most, swooning at once
> Into a sea of bliss."

When you think of pain, remember and bless

the memories of Paracelsus, and of Simpson, the discoverer of chloroform. " I precede my age," he says in the poem. There are many hints in his works that he knew a great deal more than he cared to make known. Take this example. He said : " Every peasant has seen that a magnet will attract iron. I have discovered that the magnet, besides this visible power, has another and a concealed power." Again : " A magnet may be prepared out of some vital substance that will attract vitality." Mesmer, who lived nearly 300 years after him, reaped the glory of a discovery made, as Lessing says, by the martyred fire-philosopher who died in Salzburg hospital.

From this study of a soul Mr. Browning evidently desires us to learn at least one great lesson—that neither the intellect without the heart nor the heart without the intellect will avail for the highest service of man by his brother. We are just beginning to learn that the Gospel of the Carpenter's Son is a life to be lived, not a mere creed to be believed. I am not quite sure that Mr. Browning did well to point this moral from the life of his hero. He was only unloving and unlovable when com-

bating the gross stupidity and bigoted' ignorance of his brother doctors. He seems to
have been in life and death the loving friend
of the poor, to whom when he died he left all
his goods. But the lesson of the union of
heart and head is good to learn from any
parable. Think of this. Just about the time
of Paracelsus, a company of heretics, about to
be burned at the stake, were compelled to
listen to a sermon from this text : " If I give
my body to be burned, and have not charity,
it profiteth me nothing ; " and probably the
preacher really believed he was preaching the
doctrines of Christ. Why has the Gospel of
Love survived this perverted systematic theology ? Because, after all, the human heart is
stronger than the human head.

There is a large and beautiful church in the
Roman Campagna built on such a pestilential
soil, so deadly in its effects on the atmosphere,
that it can no longer be used for worship.
Its marble pillars are entwined with luxuriant
creepers, its cracked and crumbling monuments
are garlanded with lovely southern flowers,
lilies and roses grow out of its tombs, and the
choir stalls, carved with quaint figures of de-

mons and satyrs, are beds from which spring
delicate mosses and fair ferns ; the birds build
their nests in the traceries of the beautiful
storied windows, and the lizard sports on its
marble walls, the bats haunt its dark recesses.
A solitary monk, as a penance for past sins,
says the daily mass before its moss-grown altar,
at which no worshipper but himself dares to
kneel. Yet the flowers breathe the pestilential
atmosphere uninjured, and beautify the ruins
on which they grow. " Only gradually," says
Professor Graetz, "does religion become
humanized." Had not human love, like these
fair flowers, softened and adorned the grim and
crumbling creations of a pseudo-scientific and
dogmatic theology, religion would have long
since lost its hold on modern man. To live *to
know* alone, is to miss life's end ; to live *to love*,
for art and beauty and pleasantness alone, is to
miss it just as surely as Paracelsus missed it.
" And why ? " he asks :—

" In my own heart love had not been made wise
To trace love's faint beginnings in mankind,
To know even hate is but a mask of love's,
To see a good in evil, and a hope
In ill-success ; to sympathise, be proud
Of their half reasons, faint aspirings, dim

Struggles for truth, their poorest fallacies,
Their prejudice and fears and cares and doubts ;
All with a touch of nobleness, despite
Their error, upward tending although weak,
Like plants in mines which never saw the sun,
But dream of him, and guess where he may be,
And do their best to climb and get to him.
All this I knew not, and I failed."

" And this was Paracelsus ! "

# RABBI BEN EZRA.

---

FIVE years ago a dozen ladies and gentlemen, living in one of the suburbs of London, arranged to meet together at stated intervals for the purpose of diligently studying the works of Robert Browning. They were moved to this by the fact that a short series of lectures had just been delivered in their neighbourhood by some well-known Browning scholars, notably Dr. Furnivall and Miss Hickey. The plan adopted was simply to take one of the poems in the first series of the Selections,* and go steadily through it, line by line, taking care not to let any thought pass till it was clearly understood by every member of the company. Although, with perhaps two exceptions, the friends were all strangers to the works of the great poet, it was remarked that, in the careful perusal of the poem, which was urged pre-

---

* *Selections from the Works of Robert Browning.* London : Smith, Elder & Co.

paratory for each meeting, almost every member was able to contribute something towards the elucidation and illustration of even the obscurer lines of the evening's study ; and now, looking back at those pleasant meetings, the majority of the little company would, I think, be able to say that their time and attention had been well bestowed in the efforts to master the pregnant and vigorous teaching of Mr. Browning. We began with *Rabbi Ben Ezra*, a well-known and favourite poem, which is popularly considered perhaps as one of the easiest to understand. As it is certainly a work which is very typical of Mr. Browning's philosophy, it may be questioned whether its apparent simplicity will not disappear before the serious attempt to suck each verse dry of its wonderful teaching. The fact is, as the little class soon discovered, the poem is a test of the mental attitude and capacity required to make the Browning student. If, after several perusals, a reader makes up his mind that the author of *Rabbi Ben Ezra* has something to say to him that no other writer has said so well before, let him go on with his study, in Browning he will find the teacher he has been seeking ; but if, on the contrary, the poem finds in that reader's soul no responsive sentiments starting into life, and harmonizing with its teaching, it is pretty safe to say he will never make a Browningite. It is undoubtedly one of the noblest religious poetical utterances in the language, and will repay all the thoughtful attention we may devote to it; but it is probable this may not strike the reader at the first or even the second perusal. It may be objected that we do not read poetry for the sake of solving riddles, nor for the purpose of mental gymnastics, but for the pleasures of imagination. These are not, however, valid objections to such a poem as *Rabbi Ben Ezra.* There is abundant imagination in it of the most pleasurable sort; but as it deals with the philosophy of life, it must of necessity deal with matters appertaining to the great problems of our earthly pilgrimage. Life is a riddle, after all, and there can be no greater pleasure to the thinking man than the exercise of his mental powers on the great questions of " the whence, the how, and the why." The old Rabbi, towards the close of a long and honourable life, is looking back on the way he has travelled,

and forwards towards its goal ; and as he stands
resting, as it were, to sum up the loss and gain
of life, we feel that here, at least, is no mere
dramatic utterance, but Robert Browning himself reflecting on the chief end of man, and ex-
pressing in profound philosophy what the child
says simply in the Catechism, that the chief
end of man is to know, love, and serve God in
this life, and to be happy with Him for ever in
the next.    Rabbi Ben Ezra sings in thirty-two
stanzas what the child repeats in those few
simple words.    The poem opens with a plea
for a completely developed life ; and this claim
is made throughout the whole of the poet's
teaching.    God says,—

> " A whole I planned,
> Youth shows but half."

And so old age is not the mere subsidence and
decay of powers that were once high and noble,
which are falling into ruin, but the completion,
the perfection, of the life ordained by God—

> " The last of life, for which the first was made ; "

and which, rightly understood, is actually the
best.    In the admirable antithesis of this first
stanza we have the poet's eulogium on growing

old, if happily we grow old with the noble
Rabbi—

> " Grow old along with me ! "

in the faith and high purpose which sustained
him from the outset, as his Bishop Blougram
says,—

> " Belief or unbelief
> Bears upon life, determines its whole course,
> Begins at its beginning."

So his—

> " Great aim, like a guiding star, above—
> Tasks strength, wisdom, stateliness, to lift
> His manhood to the height that takes the prize."

And so the stateliness, the wisdom, and the
strength, arrived at due completion, will—

> "Lead him at his grandest to the grave."

Again and again, like a musician reverting to
his great theme, we find, in the poet's works,
this praise of a good man's old age, as in the
*Inn Album*—

> " My life's remainder, which, say what fools will,
> Is, or should be, the best of life ; its fruit
> All tends to root and stem, and leaf and flower."

In the third verse we have another eminent

characteristic of his teaching—the purpose of
doubt in the development of soul. With
Browning everything must have its purpose.
Doubt must be good somehow or other, or we
should not find it "rapping and knocking at
and entering our souls." The point is—

> "How can we guard our unbelief?
> Make it bear fruit to us?"

And so the Rabbi says,—

> "Rather I prize the doubt
> Low kinds exist without,
> Finished and finite clods, untroubled by a spark"

As the purgatory of the thinker, he finds it
almost indispensable to the formation of the
highest intellects. He has not much opinion
of those who "solely seek and find and feast."

> "Irks care the crop-full bird?
> Frets doubt the maw-crammed beast?"

With maw-crammed, crop-full folk, Browning
has little to do; his office is with the man
who has taken the key of knowledge and fear-
lessly descended with him to unlock the dark
vaults wherein are laid the foundations of our
beliefs and the arches on which rests the
superstructure of our faith. He need not fear

to grope his way amid their dark recesses with Robert Browning for guide. With such a Great-heart he shall—

"Face the spectres of the mind, and lay them."

In the sixth verse we come upon another great article of the poet's system of philosophy —the uses of earth's roughnesses, stings, pains, and rebuffs ; not the smoothness, but the roughness of life ; not the ease, but the sting that bids us go ; not the all-pleasant things, but the joys that are three parts pain. These are the stimulants of soul growth, the mind bracers, the steps by which we mount.

Mr. Browning's healthy optimism is well exhibited in the touching lines in the seventh verse—

"What I aspired to be,
And was not, comforts me."

There are lives which succeed, though to outward seeming they may be miserable failures. It is the aspiration which makes the man, as he tells us over and over again, nowhere more grandly than in *Saul.*

"Saul, the mistake,
Saul, the failure, the ruin he seems now—and bid him awake

From the dream, the probation, the prelude, to find himself
    set
Clear and safe in new light and new life—a new harmony
    yet.

          .        .        .        .        .        .

'Tis not what man Does which exalts him, but what man
    Would do ! "

Our proper sphere is ever indicated by the
direction and intensity of our aspirations and
soul strivings.   As plants in mines, that never
see the sun, tend upwards towards the light, so
the inner aim shows the true man.

> " Better have failed in the high aim as I,
>     Than vulgarly in the low aim succeed,"

he says in the *Inn Album.*   The same truth
is emphasized in *Fifine at the Fair :—*

> " I gather heart through just such conquests of the soul,
>     Through evolution out of that which, on the whole,
>     Was rough, ungainly, partial accomplishment, at best."

The world is very hard upon the failures,
and seldom gives credit even for the working,
however good, of the sum which does not come
out right.   But happily God does not judge
after this manner.

> " All men strive, and who succeed ? "

> "What hand and brain rest ever paired?
> What heart alike conceived and dared?
> What act proved all its thought had been?
> What will but felt the fleshly screen?"
> *The Last Ride Together.*

We have the same idea in another form, in the concluding lines of *A Grammarian's Funeral*:—

> "That low man goes on adding one to one,
> His hundred's soon hit:
> The high man, aiming at a million,
> Misses an unit."

The tower at Pisa, not falling, but vainly trying to lift its head, is nobler, with all its imperfection, than our Monument, which at least is perpendicular, though, as Pope said,—

> "Like a tall bully, it lifts the head and lies."

The noblest commentary on the eighth verse is Lord Tennyson's, *By an Evolutionist*, which commences with the daring line,—

> "The Lord let the house of a brute to the soul of a man."

Browning asks,—

> "What is he but a brute
> Whose flesh hath soul to suit?"

And his teaching is, that the brute's office is first to help soul.

"In our flesh grows the branch of this life, in our soul it bears fruit."

"The angel in man is not to do homage to the brute in man," as Dewey finely says; yet Browning scruples not to defend the body from the macerations of the ascetic; and man, —the whole man,—has a right to the "body at its best." Tennyson says,—

"Hold the sceptre, human soul, and rule thy promise of the brute."

Yes, rule—not destroy! Neither pamper nor crush. "All good things are ours." What wonder the purpose fails, the will is so weak in a large proportion of our habitual criminal and pauper classes! Go over one of our great convict prisons with an artist and an anthropologist, measure the heads of the criminals, take stock of their brain capacity, study the facial angles, the formation of the head, hear the artist compare the shape and aspect of the prisoners' frame with those of his models, ask the anatomist to point you out the deficiencies which he finds in their development, and you will say that, in the greater proportion by far, the inhabitants of the dismal abodes of crime were so heavily handicapped by nature that they never could have had a fair start in life. The first necessity of a man's soul is a "body at its best." When statesmen and tax-payers get to know all that is meant by this line of the poet's, a modified form at least of Christian Socialism will not be far off.

> "How good to live and learn!"
> "Earth being so good, would heaven seem best?"
> *The Last Ride Together.*

> "O world, as God has made it! All is beauty,
> And knowing this is love, and love is duty."
> *The Guardian Angel.*

> "How good is man's life, the mere living! how fit to employ
> All the heart and the soul and the senses for ever in joy."
> *Saul.*

This is how Browning all through his works, the healthiest of modern poets, speaks of life. In the whole of his books there is not a single whine; even dramatically, he could not have made his most despicable character utter such a question as, "Is life worth living?"

When it comes to talking like that, there must
be a screw loose somewhere. We expect a
nineteenth-century poet to be sane. Very fair
poetry has, we believe, been scribbled by
patients on the walls of a lunatic asylum. Mad
poetry may be written, but the day has gone
by when it will be read. None but a mentally
rickety man or woman ever asked, " Is life
worth living?" with any expectation of getting
a negative answer; but Browning's mind pre-
supposes Browning's body, and that was "body
at its best." To him who longs morbidly for
death, Browning sternly says, " Hast thou ever
truly lived ? " He thanks God that he was a
man when he sees the whole design, but it is
the complete manhood for which he is thank-
ful. He demands that each element in human
nature shall be allowed fair play ; it is unfair
predominance which spoils the man. Control,
restraint, no waste of any faculty.

> " Since require Thou wilt
> At my hand its price, we say !
> What the price is, who can say ? "

To understand the full teaching of verse
eleven, we should read *Fra Lippo Lippi*, the
yearning for rest is so natural, the flesh is so

pleasant; but we want patience, not rest, stimulating to go on—not "by-path-meadows" and "rose-meshes." We are not to expect to make headway by despising the flesh, neither are we to renounce it as a thing accursed; we must accept life on its own terms, as he says in *Sordello,*—

> " To no mad wings transmute
> These limbs of mine."

Life's cup must be quaffed to its extreme dull dregs, and as Fra Lippo Lippi says,—

> " This world's no blot for us,
> Nor blank; it means intensely, and means good.
> To find its meaning is my meat and drink."

Life may err as gravely by being over-spiritual as over-worldly; Browning's mind is too healthy to run into either extreme. The best commentary on the thirteenth verse is that wonderful death-song of Paracelsus in the fifth Act, where the martyr of science, dying in Salzburg hospital, tells of the origin of man from lower forms, and prophesies of the time when,—

> " In completed man begins anew
> A tendency to God."

> " Man is not Man as yet,"—

But he is for ever removed from the brute,—

"A god, though in the germ."

Facing death, "fearless and unperplexed," he stood waiting for the last fight, as we see him in *Prospice*, in *Rabbi Ben Ezra*, and notably in the epilogues of his later volumes.   In the last page of *Ferishtah's Fancies*, dated December 1st, 1883, we find the noble old man waiting God's "Come!" as a soldier, forward face, no sneak lagging behind, battling it like a man, not boy-like sulking or whining; and so through all his works, till we read the last line his manly pen has traced for us, published to the world on his very death day, still the same,— "one who never turned his back, but marched breast forward," crying, "Speed,—fight on! Strive and thrive!"

The unity of Browning's teaching, and its consistency from first to last, is one of the secrets of his great power.   As the soul is held by Browning to be eternal, this life is considered as but the preparatory school-time, the first lessons in warfare are given here; but Browning's Future Life is no Mohammed's Paradise;   in   the   There,   as   in   the   here, he tells us, in his last line of his last poem, we—

"Fight on, fare ever There as here !"

So, in the fourteenth verse of *Rabbi Ben Ezra*, he tells us we shall not be perplexed in our next " brave adventure,"—

"What weapons to select, what armour to indue."

Those of us who saw him laid to rest in the old abbey pictured him going out "from the great deep to the great deep," passing "to be king among the dead," not with grievous wound as Arthur, but full armed, sword in hand, face forward, fighting to the last, unscathed through all. " There is nothing," says Seneca, "more disgraceful than that an old man should have nothing to produce as a proof that he has lived long except his years." The Rabbi having proved the Past, faces the Future judicially. He has accumulated great store of experience, and he estimates the various points of the life-struggle of the past at their true value. Herein he finds no cause for shame ; there were errors enough, but they were merely the uncouth acts of the pupil learning his business ; the proof that he has really lived is found, not in an

addition sum, but in the real work done; the
Man evolved, the God in the germ.

The lesson enforced in the nineteenth verse
is the Gospel of Work. " In God's name produce something," said Carlyle. We come
nearest to God the Creator when we engage
in true work, which is ever sacred and eternal.
" Strive *towards* making," says Browning.
" Man is purposed to grow, and forced to try
and make, else fail to grow." If impossible
always to grasp and gain the good beyond, in
this is no failure. The mere attempt is growth.
He sets all this out in a wonderful passage
in the *Ring and the Book*, vol. i. lines 710
to 760. Man repeats God's process in his due
degree; if he cannot create, he may at least
resuscitate; he may complete the incomplete,
breathe on and relume the half-quenched
wicks of the lamp. This is the true purpose
of youth—its uncouth attempts at making, prepare for an old age exempt from strife, blessed
with the privilege of knowledge. Then may
he wait the end, and not be afraid. Strive to
the end; yes, not blindly, but assured of
victory. Almost the last words uttered by
the late Lord Shaftesbury were these : " De-

pend on it, we shall beat the devil yet, if we only keep on to the end, and never despair." Youth strives for mere necessity of exercise ; that is better than repose. The strife of the Rabbi's age was the strife of "Prospice" for the victory all but assured, the prize all but grasped. Then comes the judgment on the life's work. The vulgar mass men call "work" will often make a very poor figure beside the immature instincts and the unsure purposes which then for the first time will be accurately weighed and measured. "The vulgar mass" took the eye, and had its price ; rode in its gilded car, and wore its crown ; had its monument, and stands on our roll of fame ; had all its reward, and enjoyed all its good things ; and the world's coarse thumb and finger plumbed its value, estimated it all without a pause. So much to its mind was it, there was no room for hesitation ; its price to the last farthing was paid. But the great thoughts which could never be crystallized into a single poor act the world could ever be brought to notice, the ethereal fancies, the noble aspirations, the longing after God—

R. B.                                              P

" All I could never be,
All men ignored in me ;
This I was worth to God."

And God's measure is not coarse, and His
balance weighs the evanescent fancy, and His
rod measures the depth of the feeling that never
struggled upwards into one poor act, and it is
all there, and the record which cannot err puts
down the mighty from his seat, and exalts the
humble and the meek.

" Was I, the world arraigned, right ? " Very
likely. " Were they, my soul disdained,
right ? " Perhaps. Truth and peace shall
come at last. Some one once said—I remember
not where I saw it—" When the British public
feels elevated and sublime, it comes to Westminster Abbey to look at the tombstones,
and it says, ' Here are *my* great men ; they
worked for me. I bought them ; I paid for
them.' " The British public fully appreciates
no work till a handsome tombstone assures it
that it is safe in doing so ; then it takes the eye,
then its price is paid. It will flatter itself before
long that it has even bought and paid for its
Browning ! The great lesson of the true estimate of that for which the world's balance is

too coarse an instrument, is that which bids
us remember that our aspirations, our ways of
life and manner of thought, our seeking after
love, and our efforts for good, are all so much
real gain for our individual souls, and have an
eternal value quite beyond the passing delight
and the internal satisfaction they bring, or even
the good contributed to the world without.

> " There shall never be one lost good !
> What was, shall live as before."
> " All we have lived or hoped for or dreamed of good shall
>     exist :
> Not its semblance, but itself."

" All I could never be," is the epitaph on
many a noble man and woman perished in the
cruel east wind of the blighting, hard world.
This demands immortality, or life is a poor
cheat.

The concluding verses of the poem are
occupied with the elaboration of the beautiful
metaphor of the potter's wheel—Time phe-
nomenal, God eternal ; changing earth, God
and soul alone standing sure. That which
really IS lasts ever.

> " Time's wheel runs back or stops : potter and clay en-
>     dure."

But the change is good for us.  It is well
that the wheel does turn ; by that we are
shaped ; by that movement "we draw beauty
into our heart's core."

> " Rejoice that man is hurled
> From change to change unceasingly,
> His soul's wings never furled ! "

So all the plastic circumstance of this life's
dance is just that in which the potter has
fixed us to give our souls their bent.   God
planted us just where we grow, and blossom
and fruit must be drawn, not from the meadow
on the other side of the road, or from the
mountain beyond the valley, but from the soil
now about our roots, and the air and rain and
sun above us playing on our leaves and
branches.   Yet, fixed as we are, the circumstance is neither iron nor adamant, but plastic
for us, for we are not vegetables, but men.
The potter's wheel is intended to mould men
into cups for the Master's lips.   Not in the
bowl, not in the stem, with all their quaint
device and laughing loves, are found the proper
uses of a cup ; not the uncouth beginnings of
life, not the ornament, but the perfected cup, to
slake the Master's thirst.   These are the uses

of a cup, flawed, strained, warped, alas! But take, use, and amend Thy work—Thou, not I, the potter! Quaint old Francis Quarles, in one of his emblems, has a prayer which I think must have been in Mr. Browning's mind when he wrote these powerful verses :—

> "Eternal Potter, whose blest hands did lay
> My coarse foundation from a sod of clay,
> Thou know'st my slender vessel's apt to leak :
> Thou know'st my brittle temper's prone to break :
> Are my limbs brazil, or my flesh of oak?
> Oh, mend what Thou hast made, what I have broke :
> Look, look with gentle eyes, and in Thy day
> Of vengeance, Lord, remember I am clay."

# BROWNING AND VIVISECTION.

As we have seen, Mr. Browning's sympathy with the science of his time was both wide and well-informed  He was not its slave, was neither blind to its necessary defects as an efficient substitute for religious faith, nor willing to concede all that is demanded in its name.  He was early associated with Miss Frances Power Cobbe in her noble and self-sacrificing efforts to expose scientific cruelty in that form especially which is known as Vivisection, or the cutting into live animals for physiological and pathological investigation. Mr. Browning was to the last a Vice-President of the Victoria Street Society for the Protection of Animals, and he always expressed the utmost abhorrence of the practices which it opposes.

The following letter was written by Mr. Browning on the occasion of the presentation of the memorial to the R.S.P.C.A. in 1875 :—

19, WARWICK CRESCENT, W.
*Dec. 28th*, 1874.

DEAR MISS COBBE,—

I return the petition unsigned, for the one good reason—that I have just signed its fellow forwarded to me by Mrs. Leslie Stephen.* You have heard, " I take an equal interest with yourself in the effort to suppress vivisection." I dare not so honour my mere wishes and prayers as to put them for a moment beside your noble acts; but this I know, I would rather submit to the worst of the deaths, so far as pain goes, than have a single dog or cat tortured on the pretence of sparing me a twinge or two. I return the paper, because I shall be probably shut up here for the next week or more, and prevented from seeing my friends. Whoever would refuse to sign would certainly not be of the number.

Ever truly and gratefully yours,

ROBERT BROWNING.

In his poem *Tray*, the poet describes an

---

* This lady was Mr. Stephen's first wife, the daughter of Thackeray, and sister of Mrs. Richmond Ritchie.

instance of animal courage and devotion which was witnessed by one of his friends in Paris.

A little girl fell into the river. None of the spectators went to her rescue; but a dog plunged into the water and saved the child; then, to the astonishment of the bystanders, dived again, and after battling with the stream, appeared with the child's doll in his mouth, brought that to land also, and then trotted off as if he had done nothing worthy of praise.

> "'Up he comes with the child, see, tight
> In mouth, alive too, clutched from quite
>     A depth of ten feet—twelve, I bet !
>     Good dog ! What, off again ! There's yet
> Another child to save ?    All right !
>
> ' How strange we saw no other fall !
> It's instinct in the animal.
>     Good dog ! But he's a long while under :
>     If he's got drowned I should not wonder—
> Strong current, that against the wall !
>
> ' Here he comes, holds in his mouth this time
> —What may the thing be ? Well, that's prime !
>     Now, did you ever ?   Reason reigns
>     In man alone, since all Tray's pains
> Have fished – the child's doll from the slime !'·
>
> And so, amid the laughter gay,
> Trotted my hero off,—old Tray,—
>     Till somebody, prerogatived

With reason, reasoned : ' Why he dived,
His brain would show us, I should say.

' John, go and catch—or, if needs be, ʿ
Purchase that animal for me !
  By vivisection, at expense
  Of half-an-hour and eighteenpence,
How brain secretes dog's soul, we'll see ! ' "

Here the poet ridicules the idea that the
seat of the soul can be discovered by a more
intimate knowledge of the brain, and bitterly
satirizes the heartlessness and base ingratitude
of our physiologists who use the dog, notwithstanding his intimate relationship to and friend-
ship for man, as the material for their cruel experiments in the physiological laboratory. Not
only did Mr. Browning think this to be useless
and wicked, but he denounced it as cowardly
even if it could be proved to be useful. In his
last volume, published on the day of his death,
there is a poem called *Arcades Ambo*, which is
a delicate satire on the cowardice of those who
advocate vivisection on the ground of its utility
in medicine. The poet says that the man who
would have animals tortured for the relief of
his own pain is as great a poltroon as the
soldier who runs away in battle when the balls

fly about.    Both shun death, and both are
cowards to be scorned.

The advocate of vivisection says :—

"—Shun death at all risks ?   Well, at some !
    True, I myself, sir, though I scold
The cowardly, by no means come
    Under reproof, as overbold
—I, who would have no end of brutes
    Cut up alive to guess what suits
My case and save my toe from shoots."

When recently I asked Mr. Browning to become a patron of the new hospital to be called
the Shaftesbury, and which is to be started for
the treatment of patients on principles which
exclude vivisection, I received from him the
following letter :—

29, DE VERE GARDENS, W.
*August 27th*, 1889.

MY DEAR DR. BERDOE,—

I shall be delighted if the association of my
name with those of the patrons of the proposed
scheme for an Anti-Vivisectionist Hospital be
of the least service in so holy a cause.

Do permit me to take the opportunity of
saying how grateful I am to you on other
grounds.

Ever truly yours,

ROBERT BROWNING.

**29, DE VERE GARDENS.**

Aug. 27. '89.   W.

My dear Dr. Berdoe,

I shall be delighted if the asso:
2ciation of my name with those of
the Patrons of the proposed scheme
for an Anti-vivisectionist Hospital
be of the least service in so holy
"a cause"

Do permit me to take the op:
=portunity of saying how grateful
I am to you on other grounds.

Ever truly yours

Robert Browning

Some persons affect to see in this attitude of the great poet proof that he was not imbued with the scientific spirit, that his early religious training and connections had made him afraid of science ; but surely a man is no more expected to follow science blindfold than to adopt the same behaviour towards all the claims made for blind adhesion in the name of religion. It would appear though that Science can be quite as exacting as religion in her claims for the entire allegiance of her followers. Mr. Browning resented the arrogance of both. His anti-vivisection sympathies were no mere philanthropic "fads," no mere amiable fancy adopted by chance, or arising simply from kindness of heart. They were demanded by his ethical system, and were the direct outcome of his Philosophy of Life. Love is the one word which sums up his moral teaching ; love to God reflected in the Service of Man. To have excluded anything which lives and suffers from the influence of this Love, would have offered violence to the principles which animated every line of his works, from *Pauline* to *Asolando.* Paracelsus and Sordello both failed from want of love, the former especially, by elevating knowledge to the royal throne of Love, which should dominate the human heart.

"I seemed to long
At once to trample on, yet save mankind."

But mankind can never be saved by its tramplers! Love alone, the sole good of life on earth, can be the Saviour of Mankind ; and he who violates this principle in any degree, just by so much tramples on mankind. The torture of living animals could never therefore be to Browning the royal road to the Art of Healing. To harden a human heart till the vivisector was fully equipped, was to destroy the very principle which alone, according to his theory, could make a true servant of man. To inflict pain on an innocent animal, that " some fancied good to man " might accrue, was to work with the devil's tools, and to heap up gold that would turn out at last to be but withered leaves.

# THE BROWNING SOCIETY.

I CANNOT conclude this little work without some reference to the Browning Society, in which I have taken an active interest almost from its foundation in 1881. "For eight years and a half it has challenged—and in a certain sense compelled—attention to the great merits of the works of the late poet;" and it would be impossible to deny that "it has had some share in effecting the marked change in opinion concerning them." Ten years ago, Browning was ridiculed by every scribbler, and contemned by all the press; now he lies in Poet's Corner in Westminster Abbey. Immediately after the Browning Society was started by Dr. Furnivall and Miss E. H. Hickey, the sale of the poet's works was immensely stimulated, and the volumes that were lying neglected on the publishers' shelves speedily got into circulation; and little wonder. When Mr. Nettleship, Professor Westcott, Archdeacon Farrar, the Revs. Llewellyn Davies, Professor Johnson, Dr. Hiram Corson, Mr. Barnett Smith, Mr. Moncure Conway, the Hon. Roden Noel, Dr. Peter Bayne, Mrs. Sutherland Orr, Mr. Cotter Morrison, Rev. H. R. Haweis, Mr. Holman Hunt, and a host of other men and women famous in Literature and Art lent their valuable aid to the Society, and told the public why the study of Browning was peculiarly good for the men and women of the present day, people began to see that the cheap scribblers of the press had probably misled them, and

were induced to read for themselves. Then
the Browning Society in its turn was attacked.
It was said that a number of infatuated no-
bodies met together to adulate the poet, and
cover him with their uncritical praise. As a
matter of fact, the members of the Browning
Society simply met to study the poet's works,
as a class might meet to study Thucydides or
Homer at College. No one was pledged to in-
discriminate admiration of Browning, any more
than a student at Cambridge is pledged to
admiration of the Greek author he reads in
class. We met to learn, feeling sure that the
poet was profound and interesting enough to
repay the trouble we were put to in the process; and we are doing the same now. We
meet once a month from October to June
(except in December) on the 4th Friday of
every month at 8 p.m., at University College,
Gower Street, W.C., for the hearing and
discussion of a Paper or Address on some
of Browning's poems, or his characteristics.
The best Papers, and reports of the discussions,
are printed and sent to all the members. The
subscription is 21s. a year. Our President is
Dr. F. J. Furnivall, 3, St. George's Square,
Primrose Hill, London, N.W., and names of
those who are willing to join the Society should
be sent to him. For my own part, I shall be
happy to answer any questions, and to give
any information about the Society, if inquirers
will address me at Tynemouth House, Victoria
Park Gate, London, N.E.